Theories of Childhood

Also by Carol Garhart Mooney

Swinging Pendulums: Cautionary Tales for Early Childhood Education

Theories of Attachment: An Introduction to Bowlby, Ainsworth, Gerber, Brazelton, Kennell, and Klaus

Theories of Practice: Raising the Standards of Early Childhood Education

Use Your Words: How Teacher Talk Helps Children Learn

Theories of Childhood

An Introduction to Dewey, Montessori, Erikson, Piaget, and Vygotsky

Second Edition

Carol Garhart Mooney

Redleaf Press®
www.redleafpress.org
800-423-8309

Published by Redleaf Press
10 Yorkton Court
St. Paul, MN 55117
www.redleafpress.org

First edition published 2000. Second edition 2013.
Cover design by Jim Handrigan
Author photo by Jeff Klapes
Excerpt on page 56 is from "Linking Brain Principles to High-Quality Early Childhood Education," Exchange 202 (Nov/Dec): 8–11, by Stephen Rushton and Anne Juola-Rushton. Copyright © 2011 Exchange Press, Inc. Reprinted with permission.
Photograph of Maria Montessori on page 35 © Hulton-Deutsch Collection/CORBIS
Photograph of Erik Erikson on page 53 © Ted Streshinsky/CORBIS
Printed in the United States of America

Library of Congress Cataloging-in-Publication Data
Mooney, Carol Garhart.
    Theories of childhood : an introduction to Dewey, Montessori, Erikson, Piaget, and Vygotsky / Carol Garhart Mooney. — Second edition.
        pages cm
    Summary: "Examine the work of five groundbreaking education theorists: John Dewey, Maria Montessori, Erik Erikson, Jean Piaget, and Lev Vygotsky—in relation to early childhood. Theories of Childhood, Second Edition, provides a basic introduction to each theorist and explains the relationship of theory to practice and its impact on real children, teachers, and classrooms" — Provided by publisher.
    Includes bibliographical references and index.
    ISBN 978-1-60554-138-9 (pbk.)
    ISBN 978-1-60554-248-5 (e-book)
    1. Early childhood education—Philosophy. 2. Child development—Philosophy.
I. Title.
LB1139.23.M64 2013
305.231—dc23
                                    2012032505

Printed on acid-free paper   U15-09

For Jeannette Stone, mentor and friend

Contents

Acknowledgments

THIS BOOK WAS WRITTEN LATE at night and on weekends, sandwiched between family and work life. It bears my name only, but, as I'm sure it is with most books, this one was a group effort.

To begin with, the thinking and framework for this review of early childhood theory was a collaborative effort with my friend and colleague Jeannette Stone. It was always "our" project!

The manuscript was refined thanks to the computer skills and energy of Marguerite Shanelaris. I am grateful to so many colleagues at New Hampshire Head Start and the New Hampshire Child Care Association for sharing their stories and classrooms with me. When I grew weary, I was forced back on track by the special friendship and support of Jay Munson, Sue Cloutier, and Pat Meattey. I am grateful to my many students at the Granite State College and the New Hampshire Community Technical Colleges who convinced me of the need for the book.

I appreciate the opportunity Redleaf Press has given me to bring the seed of this book to fruition. My editor, Beth Wallace, convinced me I could get it done and offered humor and support along the way.

Finally, I thank my children:

Sean, for decades of support of my writing and the book on Vygotsky.

Brian, for offering humor when I needed it and for forcing me to enter the computer age.

Tom, for downloading the research and late-night computer assistance.

Erin, for accepting a preoccupied mom and loving me anyway.

We're done!

Carol Garhart Mooney
Manchester, New Hampshire
June 2000, updated July 2012

Introduction to the Second Edition

FIFTEEN YEARS AGO WHEN I BEGAN WORK on the first edition of *Theories of Childhood*, I knew it was a good idea. I had been a practitioner and college instructor for many years and knew that parents, child care teachers, providers, and students all increasingly struggled with what to do with the children.

I never expected the response to the book that I have enjoyed in the past decade. At conferences and training sessions, I am frequently approached by students who say they never "got" theory until they were forced to read my book in college. I have appreciated feedback from the many community college, university, and graduate school instructors who thank me for creating a usable text for beginners.

It is interesting that I have received comments and letters from many readers for whom English is not their native language. These practitioners have thanked me for helping them transition to caregiving in the United States. It is both humbling and gratifying to think that my own theory and practice struggles have helped colleagues to frame both for their daily work with children.

It is also interesting to me that there was some question at the time about using the Margaret Mead quote in the introduction. Objections were twofold. The editor did not like that the quote was from 1963 (still relevant?). And the source (*Redbook* magazine), we would mostly agree, is not a credible research tool for writing a textbook. I was new to the world of writing textbooks, and to me, Margaret Mead was credible wherever and whenever she made comments about the human condition.

Today, with over 75,000 copies in circulation, I am more confident about Mead's words and my insistence that we use

1

them. The teacher who most affected me in my undergraduate years made a similar comment to Mead's in his existential philosophy course. "This course," he was known to say, "attracts those who want a podium. If you have something to say . . . it best be said in a way that my great-aunt Gertrude, who has only a third-grade education, can read it and understand it." A good rule of thumb for sharing important information is to use simple, direct language.

The mistake I made was assuming that the piece of my contract that said I would be willing to update as needed would ever be "called in." It is a source of some humor both at Redleaf and my house that I had quite intentionally chosen theorists who were quite dead. I figured if I was able to state the theorists' perspective in a clear, straightforward manner, offering classroom examples . . . what more could be done? It's not like there would be additional work to discuss.

Today this seems extraordinarily naive to me. The 1990 National Teacher of the Year, Janis T. Gabay, told audiences, "I offer my students as many ideas as I can by showing them through literature that there is nothing that has not already been felt, experienced, or thought, but much to be discovered in a new way" (Council of Chief State School Officers [CCSSO], accessed 2012).

The technological changes alone to our daily lives in the past decade are astounding. Then there are changes in science, medicine, educational psychology, women's studies, and family studies. Over the past thirty years, children have been driven from the natural world by the advances of technology, fear (for example, "stranger danger," natural disasters), and even classroom messages meant to raise their concerns about the world's future (for example, global warming). This phenomenon has been termed "nature-deficit disorder." In his book *Last Child in the Woods*, author Richard Louv writes, "Nature-deficit disorder describes the human costs of alienation from nature, among them: diminished use of the senses, attention difficulties, and higher rates of physical and emotional illnesses" (2008, 36). Additionally, if children are not given opportunities to explore and embrace the natural world, who will take care of it in the future? And a decade ago, most of us didn't pay much attention to the ethnocentric (characterized by or based on the attitude that one's own group is superior) nature of many of our considerations regarding children and families in the United States. We interpret all learning with a much broader lens as we consider culture, changing times, the importance of time in nature, and practices we didn't know existed even a decade ago.

It is this spirit of "discovering in a new way" and interpreting through a broader lens and application to a new generation of young children that I offer this second edition of *Theories of Childhood*. I hope to maintain the simplicity and directness readers have appreciated while taking a fresh look at our theoretical foundations in an increasingly rapidly changing world.

Introduction to the First Edition

Raising healthy children is a labor-intensive operation. Contrary to the news from the broader culture, most of what children need, money cannot buy. Children need time and space, attention, affection, guidance, and conversation. They need sheltered places where they can be safe as they learn what they need to know to survive.

—Mary Pipher

IT ISN'T ANYONE'S IMAGINATION THAT WORKING with American children is getting harder and harder. Despite our attempts at optimism and the old lyrics "Why can't they be like we were, perfect in every way—what's the matter with kids today?" every experienced educator knows that the job was easier three decades ago. There are so many theories about why this is so that the topic could fill volumes. At a conference of educators at Harvard University, Jerome Kagan (1998) pointed out that in addition to the impact of both *heredity* (genes inherited from our birth parents) and the *environment* (people and places affecting our experiences after birth), psychologists are seeing more and more how society and culture at large affect growth and development.

What factors in American society affect the growth and development of our children? We live in one of the more violent countries of the developed world. Many Americans feel it is not safe to walk alone in their own neighborhood at night. This concern is well-founded. According to the Sentencing Project, a nonprofit agency devoted to improving the justice system, the crime rate in the United States exceeds that of most other nations (Siegel 1998).

5

Media influences and consumerism are often not in the best interest of our children. In the past forty years, more than a thousand studies on the effects of media and film violence have been conducted. In the past decade, the American Academy of Pediatrics, the American Medical Association, the American Academy of Child and Adolescent Psychiatry, and the National Institute of Mental Health have separately reviewed many of these studies. Each of these reviews has reached the same conclusion: television violence leads to real-world violence (New Hampshire Pediatric Society Newsletter, n.d.).

Family and community life have changed dramatically in the last fifty years. Much of the public discussion of these changes has focused on the negative. People express fear that the family is endangered. Campaign slogans call for a return to family values. In *The Way We Never Were*, Stephanie Coontz points out that trying to solve today's challenges to family life through a return to "traditional" family forms is pointless (1992). Americans, she writes, cherish a myth of stable, happy families that exist primarily in the minds of those who indulge in nostalgia. Families in every era have dealt with poverty, stress, death, illness, and emotional misunderstandings between family members. Child abuse, racism, and the inequities of class and gender are constants throughout our nation's history. Nostalgia for "the good old days" is not an answer, but addressing the changes of our times is necessary. Our challenge is to find adequate and creative ways to adapt to these changes.

Workplaces and community organizations have not kept pace with the changes. For example, numerous community organizations for children continue to hold events such as "father/daughter dances" or "father/son campouts," ignoring the fact that fewer than half of all American families resemble the stereotypical family of two opposite-gender married parents with children living in a single household. Similarly, many schools have not creatively adapted their parent involvement components to match the lives of dual-career or single-parent families. Failure to adapt to these social changes stresses our children.

Fifty years ago, projections were made that filling our leisure hours would be the challenge for most Americans in the 1990s. This has not proven to be true. Adults work more hours than ever. The Harris Poll reports that since 1973, free time has fallen nearly 40 percent, from a median figure of twenty-six hours a week to slightly under seventeen hours. At the same time, research shows that employed hours have risen for Americans in all income categories (Schor 1991). We spend less time with family and friends. The debates of the 1980s over quality time versus quantity time have disappeared. Today, for many, it is a stretch to find *any* time together!

By now, I'm sure the reader is asking, "What does all of this have to do with Piaget and Erikson?" Teachers in early childhood programs spend many hours discussing child and family struggles. Many of the teachers I talk with are discouraged. "The behavior problems are too much to handle," they tell me. Some of them blame parents. Some even make statements like, "If parents don't want to care for their kids, then why do they have them?" This attitude usually comes from the frustration of having daily interactions with children in pain. When we can't make it better, we want someone to blame, and parents are an easy target. Many parents are stressed too. They know their long hours are taking a toll on family life. Like teachers, they often don't know what to do to make it better.

This is where Erikson, Piaget, and the other theorists come in. When I ask teachers what they learned in college that might help them respond to children under stress, many of them just laugh. Some make comments such as "I could never keep all of those theorists straight" or "That textbook approach doesn't work once you're in a real classroom." Teachers will say, "Now, which one was he?" or "Wasn't Piaget the cognitive theory?" but rarely pause to reflect on how understanding child development theory might benefit their day-to-day classroom practices. The purpose of this small text is to look for those benefits.

Joining Theory to Practice

Anthropologist and teacher Margaret Mead said in *Redbook* magazine in 1963, "If one cannot state a matter clearly enough so that an intelligent twelve-year-old can understand it, one should remain within the cloistered walls of the University and laboratory until one gets a better grasp of one's subject matter." The field of early childhood education needs to listen to this wisdom. "I need to drop this course," a student of mine told me recently. "I'm a full-time student, the single mother of a three-year-old, and I work at Pizza Hut on weekends. I don't have the time or patience to figure out what this means!" She thrust her child development textbook onto my desk and pointed to a highlighted passage in the introductory chapter. It read: "The improvement of research tends to increase divergence in the treatment of evidence and to multiply mystification in the interpretation of specific findings. As research on a problem matures, the angles of vision multiply."

I shared with her my memorized interpretation. "It means studying children is really complicated. The more we learn, the more there is to understand about a single topic."

The student looked annoyed. "Well, why can't they just say that?" she asked. Then, in a sad and quiet voice, she added, "When I see words that I've never even heard of, I get discouraged and think I'm crazy to be going to college. The director at my center told me all that theory won't help me once I'm working with kids anyway."

8

As a teacher of child development, I am always alarmed when students share these stories, which they do frequently. To leap from disregarding difficult texts that do a poor job of introducing the subject to disregarding the importance of theory in shaping practice seems a huge mistake. Knowing the theoretical foundations of early childhood education is critical to providing quality early care and education.

Not everyone agrees with me. A few years ago a survey of child care directors was done in my state to guide the investment of training dollars. Many directors responded that they didn't care if teachers knew who Vygotsky or Erikson were, but that they wanted them to know what to do when the children were hitting or biting each other. The point these directors missed is that teachers who know what to do when children are hitting or biting are teachers who understand child development. Many of the directors interviewed said such things as "When I hire those college students, they are full of theory but don't know what to do in the classroom. I'd rather hire someone with no college but a true enjoyment of young children." We need teachers who have both a true enjoyment of children and a true understanding of how they grow and learn. It seems that we have not been successful at presenting child development as a usable tool for working with young children more effectively. Perhaps we need to take a different approach to introducing theory and its practice to the beginning student or teacher.

It is true that most of us chuckle when we say, "Well, in theory . . . ," because we all expect gaps between any theory and the way we are able to apply that theory in real life. But these gaps are part of our growing understanding of the complexity of growth and development. They are inevitable. This is not a good enough reason for practitioners to dismiss theory as "irrelevant" to their day-to-day work with children.

Jargon does not help students to grasp the important ideas of Piaget or Erikson. Memorizing names and stages out of context does not build the bridge we need between child development and children. I know that too many classrooms offer this textbook approach to theory, because when I ask teachers what they remember about child development theories from their college classes, too many of them respond, "Very little!" Others will tell me that they could never remember whether Erikson was the one who talked about feelings and Piaget about thought or the other way around. I can picture these students chanting, "Piaget, Swiss psychologist, cognitive development theory," as one might memorize state capitals and major rivers. Given this kind of introduction to theory, it is no wonder so many directors say, "Just send me someone who has good sense about kids!"

As directors struggle with staffing shortages and inadequately prepared teachers, however, it is more important to them that teachers know basic development information, such as that babies always need to be held during feeding. Teachers may not need to know that Erik Erikson was born in Germany and brought us the psychosocial theory of development, but they will do their jobs better if they know that holding babies while they are being fed helps the children to develop trust in grown-ups. Theory needs to be real to the developing teacher. It needs to be tested in practice and adapted to the realities of individual children and classrooms. This ongoing process is what builds the bridge between theory and practice. When directors and teachers see how understanding child development theory makes their days with children smoother, their jobs easier, and their programs stronger, then they will value this knowledge.

About This Book

Theories of Childhood is a practitioner's manual as well as a college textbook. It is designed for the person working with young children who wants to better understand how children think and act and how to be more effective with them. It begins with a discussion of the interactive nature of theory and practice that is necessary to make either meaningful. It includes information about and reflection on the work of five of the major contributors to the body of knowledge upon which our best practices in early childhood education are based. It is a basic introduction and is not intended to be academic or scholarly. I'm hoping to whet the appetite of those interested in the relationship of theory to practice and its impact on real children, teachers, and classrooms. For this reason, each chapter concludes with discussion questions and suggestions for further reading.

The stories shared here are from real classrooms where I have either worked or observed others at work. Each chapter provides the reader with background information on the theorist's life and work. Classroom stories are used to illustrate the point of the original writings. This is not a comprehensive introduction to the field or even to the individual theorists included. I hope that this brief introduction to early childhood's theoretical foundations will give readers a foundation for understanding how child development affects how we work with children in early childhood programs and will encourage them to go on to the more in-depth readings.

Chapter 1: John Dewey

The fundamental issue is not of new versus old education nor of progressive against traditional education but a question of what anything whatever must be to be worthy of the name education.

—John Dewey

Biography

JOHN DEWEY IS TRULY the American educator who has most influenced our thinking about education in the United States. He was born in Burlington, Vermont, in 1859. Dewey's family had farmed in Vermont for three generations. He attended the University of Vermont, where he studied philosophy. In 1884 he received a PhD at Johns Hopkins University, which led to a teaching position at the University of Michigan. While serving as a professor of philosophy there, he became friends with one of his students, Alice Chipman. They were married in 1886, and it was largely the influence of his wife that brought Dewey to the study of education. Chipman was interested in social problems and their relationship to education. Her interest was contagious, and soon she and Dewey were working together to determine the best ways to support the education of children in America.

In 1894 they moved to the University of Chicago, where Dewey took a position teaching philosophy. He found the position desirable because it was intended that he blend the teaching of philosophy with both psychology and educational

13

theory. Within two years he had established the famous laboratory school that attracted attention around the world. Dewey's Laboratory School established the University of Chicago as the center of thought on *progressive education*, the movement toward more democratic and child-centered education. Progressive education was a reaction to the rigid, more formal style of traditional education during the nineteenth century. It was considered genius by many and criticized as too radical by others. Dewey's involvement with the lab school was relatively short-lived but created, in a few years, a wealth of educational research and theory that continues to drive many of our best practices today.

In 1904, arguing with administrators over education budgets, Dewey resigned his position at the University of Chicago. He took a post at Columbia University in New York City where he continued to teach and write for another four decades. Dewey has contributed volumes of work to our knowledge base in educational psychology and theory. Much of his work is as relevant to the struggles of educators in the United States today as it was nearly a half century ago.

Dewey has contributed volumes of work to our knowledge base in educational psychology and theory.

His writings cover a broad range of topics relevant to teaching. Dewey continued writing and revising manuscripts until his death in 1952 at the age of ninety-three.

In 1899 John Dewey gave a talk to the parents of children in his school. The parents were worried about the changing times. On the edge of the industrial age, these parents of one hundred years ago were old enough to remember the "agricultural era" in the United States. They remembered when children were educated at home by watching their parents do meaningful work. They thought the new generation lacked character and values. Dewey agreed with parents that the

14

home was no longer educating children in the way it had in the past, but he gave them good counsel. "We cannot overlook the factors of discipline and of character building involved . . . but it is useless to bemoan the departure of the good old days of children's modesty, reverence, and implicit obedience, if we expect merely by bemoaning and by exhortation to bring them back" (Dewey 1899, 19, 21).

What Dewey was trying to get his parent group to understand was that change brings new problems but also new opportunities. He urged parents to think of new ways they could all find to help children learn to be socially responsible people, without trying to cling to times gone by.

At the end of the next century, teachers were struggling with the very same issues. In *Dewey's Laboratory School: Lessons for Today*, Laurel Tanner (1997) points out that a century ago Dewey asked the questions we still seek answers to in the twenty-first century: How do we best introduce children to subject matter? Should we have multiage classrooms? How can we best plan curriculum? How can supervisors support classroom teachers? How should thinking skills be taught? Significant answers to these and similar questions about teaching can be found in Dewey's many volumes. Dewey's work is echoed in the writing of many contemporary educational theorists. As we speak today of dispositions for learning, purposeful curricula, shaping experiences through well-planned environments, and many other theoretical and practical conditions of teaching, we are discussing the issues that interested Dewey and that he wrote and talked about.

Dewey played a central role in the development of—and is most associated with—the progressive education movement in the United States. In Europe, Maria Montessori and Jean Piaget were spreading the same message. These early theorists all agreed that children learn from doing and that education should involve real-life material and experiences and

15

should encourage experimentation and independent thinking. These ideas, now quite common, were considered revolutionary in Dewey's day.

Dewey's Theories

John Dewey wrote so many volumes on the philosophy and practice of education that an introductory text cannot begin to cover his contribution to our field. As a progressive educator, he shared with Lev Vygotsky, Montessori, and Piaget the central ideas of that movement: education should be child centered; education must be both active and interactive; and education must involve the social world of the child and the community. In 1897 Dewey published his philosophy of education in a document called *My Pedagogic Creed*. Here's what he said about education:

> **"True education comes through the stimulation of the child's powers by the demands of the social situations in which he finds himself" (5).** Dewey believed that children learn best when they interact with other people, working side by side and cooperatively with peers and adults.

> **"The child's own instincts and powers furnish the material and give the starting-point for all education" (6).** According to Dewey, children's interests form the basis for curriculum planning. He believed that the interests and background of each child and group must be considered when teachers plan *learning experiences*.

> **"I believe that education, therefore, is a process of living and not a preparation for future living" (8).** Dewey believed that education is part of life. He believed that as long as people are alive, they are

16

learning, and education should address what the person needs to know at the time, not prepare them for the future. Dewey thought that curriculum should grow out of real home, work, and other life situations.

"The school life should grow gradually out of the home life. . . . It is the business of the school to deepen and extend his [the child's] sense of the values bound up in his home life" (9). Dewey thought teachers must be sensitive to the values and needs of families. The values and cultures of families and communities should be reflected in and deepened by what happens at school.

"I believe, finally, that the teacher is engaged, not simply in the training of individuals, but in the formation of the proper social life" (17). Dewey believed that teachers do not only teach subject matter but also teach how to live in society. In addition, he thought that teachers do not only teach individual children but also shape the society.

It is the last piece of Dewey's pedagogic creed that is the springboard for some of his most provocative ideas. He believed that teachers need to have confidence in their skills and abilities. He believed teachers need to trust their knowledge and experience and, using both, provide appropriate activities to nurture inquiry and dispositions for learning in the children they work with.

The Teacher's Role

In *Experience and Education* (1938), Dewey writes that teachers should have more confidence when planning children's learning experiences. He writes that teachers are too afraid that instruction will infringe upon the freedom and creativity of their students. Dewey thought that children need assistance from teachers in making sense of their world.

What should this assistance look like? Dewey thought it was important for teachers to observe children and to determine from these observations what kinds of experiences the children are interested in and ready for. He thought that the educator has a serious responsibility to invest in planning and organizing for children's learning activities. In other words, he believed that it is the teacher's job to determine the curriculum based on knowledge of the children and the children's abilities. He felt that suggestions and guidance coming from thoughtful teachers, who after all have more life experience and more general knowledge than children, could be more useful to children than the ideas they arrive at by accident.

Dewey thought it was important for teachers to observe children and to determine from these observations what kinds of experiences the children are interested in and ready for.

When progressive education was criticized for allowing children too much freedom without appropriate guidance, Dewey agreed. "It is a ground for legitimate criticism, however, when the ongoing movement of progressive education fails to recognize that the problem of selection and organization of subject matter for study and learning is fundamental," he responded (Dewey 1938, 78). Dewey was saying that children need teachers to decide what is safe and also developmentally and individually appropriate for them.

Dewey was concerned that many teachers of his time were claiming to be part of progressive education merely because they departed from more traditional approaches. He recognized the danger in moving away from one direction without clearly understanding the new direction one wanted to follow. He also thought this was a very common pattern among educators. He believed there were teachers who were drawn to progressive education because they thought it would be easier. He knew that some teachers used the new ideas as justification for improvising or allowing children to choose their experiences, uninhibited by teacher planning or direction.

Dewey believed that the path to quality education is to know the children well, to build their experiences on past learning, to be organized, and to plan well. He also believed that the demands of this new method make observing, documenting, and keeping records of classroom events much more important than when traditional methods are used. Today these beliefs and many others articulated by Dewey are foundational pieces of developmentally appropriate practice and early childhood curriculum models such as emergent and constructivist.

Dewey believed that in order to provide educational experiences for children, teachers must

- have a strong base of general knowledge as well as knowledge of specific children;

- be willing to make sense of the world for children on the basis of their greater knowledge and experience; and

- invest in observation, planning, organization, and documentation.

How can Dewey's theory about the teacher's role in education guide teachers in early childhood programs? Teachers should observe children closely and plan curriculum from the children's interests and experience. And teachers shouldn't be afraid to use their knowledge of the children and the world to make sense of the world for children.

Plan Purposeful Curriculum

When visiting a group of four-year-olds, I noticed a child who spent most of her free-play time crawling about the room. She

19

would say "meow" to anyone she passed. She did not play with other children. She did not seek interaction from her teacher. She simply roamed around, meowing.

I asked the teacher about this child. "She likes to think she's a cat," the teacher said.

"Why is that?" I asked.

"I'm not sure," the teacher said.

"Does she have a cat at home?" I asked.

"I'm not sure," the teacher said again.

"Do you ever wonder what makes her do it?" I pushed.

"She really enjoys it . . . and that's enough for me," the teacher said, smiling confidently, and added, "Learning should be fun!"

This is not what Dewey meant by "teacher confidence." He said that confidence should spring from the base of knowledge that the teacher applies to classroom situations. The teacher's knowledge includes

- knowing the child (Does she have a cat?)

- individualizing curricula (Does she need to work through the death of a pet?)

- understanding the social nature of learning (How can the teacher or peers help or join her?)

- preparation for life (What is the point of this behavior? What is she learning from it that she can use as she goes through life?)

Dewey certainly believed that when children were engaged, learning was fun and exciting in and of itself. However, in this example, the teacher was content to accept "fun" as a justification for aimless activity, without trying to understand the meaning of the experience for the child. She did not build on the child's preoccupation with being a cat to extend the girl's knowledge of the world, to advance her skills, or to support her development. She did not connect the child's interest to her own broad knowledge of the world or to learning that had gone before. This is similar to the misconception among some early childhood educators today that a hands-on curriculum is enough. In *The Young Child as Scientist: A Constructivist Approach to Early Childhood Science Education*, authors Christine Chaillé and Lory Britain write, "The constructivist [teacher] sees the essential activity as what goes on in the child's head, not in his or her hands. With young children, physical activity and manipulation is often a necessary part of mental activity, but not always. . . . Children need to be active . . . and they need opportunities to manipulate and experiment with real objects. But this in itself is not the definition of a good activity" (17).

Here's a very different example. In a classroom where five-year-olds were at work, I observed some children playing with glue. At first glance, this activity seemed aimless as well as wasteful. The children had taken empty thread spools from the art area. Placing a finger under the bottom hole, they filled the spool with glue. Quickly turning it sideways, the children blew the glue out of the hole. "Wow, you did it, just like yesterday!" one child shouted exuberantly as the glue spread across the art table.

Fascinated, I was wondering what kind of curriculum the school followed when the teacher quickly intervened. "You must be showing our visitor what you did with eggs yesterday," she said. She explained that the children had been looking at decorated eggs from around the world. The teacher had shown them how the artists prepare the eggshells by blowing out the raw egg inside. Now the children's behavior made sense to me. Then the teacher said, "You really understood that process with the eggs. You have done the same thing with the spools and glue. We can't use up all of our glue, though, so I want you to put that away now. Then we can go check on our eggs from yesterday and see if they are ready to decorate."

21

This teacher knew her students well. She knew exactly what they were doing and why. She affirmed the connection between the eggs and the glue and then redirected the children to the original project. She wasn't afraid to say, "I see what you are doing. It makes sense, but let's not do it with glue. Let's get back to our eggs." Her guidance assured that the experimenting was turned from mere *experience to learning experience.* This is the confidence Dewey speaks of. It is based on knowledge of both specific children and the learning process.

Make Sense of the World for Children

Dewey also said that beyond their knowledge of children, teachers must be willing to tap their general knowledge of the world to help children make sense of their surroundings and experiences. This is a challenge for many early childhood teachers who have often been discouraged from sharing their knowledge with children.

For example, I was at a statewide gathering of Head Start teachers who were working toward their Child Development Associate Credential. As part of the seminar, teachers were reflecting on the project work they were doing with children. One teacher, Kathy, talked about her class's investigation of winter birds. The children had observed and commented on the V formation of birds flying above the play area. Their teachers explained that the birds were going south for the winter. The children knew that not all birds left New England, because there were birds coming daily to their bird feeder, and this launched the class into a project studying the birds that remained in the area during the winter.

Kathy showed the group some cardinals that the children had made. They were so realistic that at first no one guessed they were made from paper plates, painted and feathered. Several teachers also commented that they looked as if they had been made by older children.

Some of the teachers were disturbed by Kathy's presentation. "Did you use a model?" one asked.

"No," Kathy responded. "We had the children carefully observe the cardinals in the yard. We brought in lots of books with pictures and photographs, and when we set up the activity, we only set out materials and paint appropriate to making cardinals."

The discussion got more heated. "You actually did this with five-year-olds? I can't believe you would only set out red and brown paint! What if someone wanted theirs to be purple or green? Isn't this whole thing infringing on the children's creativity?" There was an explosion of questions and comments.

Kathy was tentative. Her head teacher had warned her that some of her peers might not understand or approve of the work they were doing with the class. Quietly she shared their approach. "We didn't put green paint out because there aren't green cardinals. There has been a lot of painting and drawing in other areas of the classroom, but we think of this project as scientific investigation, not creative arts. We are studying birds, what they look like, what they eat, where they live. We want the children to know more about some of the birds that live in their backyards, and we thought it was important to share accurate information. Restricting the colors they painted with for this project has actually made their study more interesting. Last week I overheard a child tell her classmate, as they stared out the window, 'That must be a blue jay. It can't be a cardinal, because they are all red!'"

This was followed by another burst of comments:

"Isn't it inappropriate to tell children what color they should use on a project?"

"If children are painting, shouldn't they use whatever color they want?"

"Well, but bird watching is different from easel painting."

"Do we really want children pointing to a pigeon and saying, 'There's a cardinal'?"

"If a child brought you a picture of an octopus and it only had six tentacles, would you correct her? Would you say, 'That's wrong; go back and add two more tentacles'?"

Kathy responded slowly and thoughtfully. "We wouldn't say 'It's wrong, go back and fix it!' but we might say some other thought-provoking things. We would have many books about sea life with drawings and photographs. We might say something like, 'Let's look at your drawing of the octopus and the pictures in *National Geographic.*' We might call attention to the fact that these creatures sure have more legs than we do! Many children would then begin counting and would realize that a real octopus has eight tentacles. This is the kind of discovery that learning is all about!"

The other teachers were not all convinced. There was a long discussion, with comments such as these:

"Process is what is important to young children."

"Each child's work should look the way she wants it to."

"This whole approach seems manipulative."

"We *never* tell children how to draw."

"This doesn't seem very developmentally appropriate!"

Kathy explained to the group that the teachers at her center had visited the *Hundred Languages of Children* exhibit. They had been amazed at some of the work done by preschoolers in Reggio Emilia, Italy. After attending project seminars, the staff had reflected on their current work with the children. Their new learning convinced them that they had been underestimating what the children were capable of. "We decided that, as teachers, our responsibility includes making sense of the world to children even if it means having them take another look at the color of birds or their two-legged horses!" she concluded.

24

Kathy's story is a good example of what Dewey meant by teachers using their greater knowledge to help the children make sense of their world. Children in her classroom have ample opportunity for unfettered creative expression, but in the study she described, children were using art as a tool for scientific investigation. By helping the children look closely at the birds they were studying and giving them the tools to make accurate representations of them, these teachers built on the children's knowledge. They

This, according to Dewey, is how teachers should use their knowledge of the world to expand children's knowledge.

helped them learn more about the birds. They also gave them skills they could use for future investigations. This, according to Dewey, is how teachers should use their knowledge of the world to expand children's knowledge.

Education versus Mis-education

Dewey avoided the either/or discussions so common to educational philosophy. He believed that the real issue is not a matter of new versus old approaches to education but rather what conditions make any experience worthy of being called "educational." Dewey insisted that education and experience are related but not equal, and that some experiences are not educational at all. He called these *mis-educative* experiences. Dewey believed that an activity is not a learning activity if it lacks purpose and organization. He criticized the more traditional formal teaching environments of the nineteenth and early twentieth centuries in which children learned information by rote and spent days reciting facts out of context. He also criticized situations in which teachers set up the learning environment and then turn children loose to explore without offering any guidance or suggestions, or randomly set up experiences without providing any unifying theme, continuity, or purpose. The situation described earlier of the teacher who thought the child pretending to be a cat was having fun and therefore learning is an example of a mis-educative experience. Dewey thought that rather than saying, "The children will enjoy this," teachers need to ask the following questions when they plan activities for children:

- How does this expand on what these children already know?
- How will this activity help this child grow?
- What skills are being developed?
- How will this activity help these children know more about their world?
- How does this activity prepare these children to live more fully?

From Dewey's perspective, an experience can only be called educational if it meets these criteria:

- It is based on the children's interests and grows out of their existing knowledge and experience.
- It supports the children's development.
- It helps the children develop new skills.
- It adds to the children's understanding of their world.
- It prepares the children to live more fully.

How can early childhood teachers be guided by Dewey's criteria for educational experiences? Do not accept "It's fun" as a justification for curriculum, but ask how an activity will support children's development and learning. Again, it is not enough for an activity to be "hands on"; it must be "minds on" as well. And teachers must invest in organization and documentation.

26

"It's Fun" Is Not Enough

Dewey believed that when people are engaged in learning something that interests them and is related to their experience, the process of learning is enjoyable. However, he also said that enjoyment on its own is not enough to make an experience educational. Teachers can use Dewey's criteria to make sure the experiences they plan for children are not only fun but also build children's learning.

For example, I once visited a classroom where children were having a make-your-own-sundae celebration. There was much excitement in the room. Children told me they could choose frozen yogurt or ice cream, sprinkles or M&Ms, and chocolate syrup or strawberries. The teacher did a survey at the end of the day asking children which flavor was their favorite. She had carefully prepared a poster. It said "Our Favorite Ice Cream!" She had cut out ice-cream cones in brown, white, and pink. The children chose cones and put their names on them. When the teacher called their names, they placed their cones next to the word *chocolate*, *vanilla*, or *strawberry*. As Zachary taped his brown cone to the chart, he smiled and said, "My favorite is Cherry Garcia."

Later I asked the teacher how she thought the activity had gone. Like so many teachers I speak with, she said, "The children really seemed to enjoy it." When I asked why she had planned this particular activity, she smiled and said, "I knew they would love it!"

Dewey would say this teacher had not done enough planning for this activity. It's unclear whether the children had expressed an interest in ice cream or how the activity built on any prior information they had. What did they already know about ice cream? What were they curious about? It's also hard to see how the activity supported children's development or helped them learn new skills. The documentation of the activity was limited to the chart, which was inaccurate—the only choices were chocolate, vanilla, and strawberry, which didn't reflect Zachary's favorite, Cherry Garcia, and his choice of a brown cone required no association of colors with flavors. In addition, by concluding an activity with a "My favorite . . ." chart, the teacher had not left the children wondering or searching for more.

Invest in Organization and Documentation

Now read about a different teacher who turned the same subject, ice cream, into a lesson Dewey would probably have identified as a learning experience. A kindergarten teacher had invited a parent to come in and share an old family recipe for peach ice cream. In preparing the children for this visit, she discovered that none of the children had ever tasted peach ice cream before. The teacher asked the children why they thought no one had ever tasted it, and she documented their answers. Here are some of them:

- "It's not at the store."
- "It's a fruit, not an ice cream."
- "I'm allergic!"
- "Chocolate is best."

The teacher asked the children to talk to their families about ice cream. "Do you eat much ice cream? Does your brother or sister have a favorite flavor? Have you ever made ice cream at home?" she asked. The next day the list of information was much longer: Anthony's dad liked Rocky Road; Alexa had gone to the Ben & Jerry's factory to watch them make ice cream; Nina's grandmother liked orange sherbet, which is sort of like ice cream but not exactly!

When the parent came in to help the children make peach ice cream, she used an old-fashioned ice cream maker.

28

It had been her grandmother's. Children took turns mixing the ingredients and turning the crank. The teacher asked the children if they thought this was how the ice cream they got at the store was made, and she documented their responses. Here are some of the things they said:

- "No—it's too slow."
- "It's not big enough to make all those ice creams."
- "They have to use gigantic bowls."
- "They don't turn the handle like this; they use a huge mixer like when my mom makes cake."

The teacher observed from these responses that the children had some ideas about how ice cream could be made in large quantities. She saw an opportunity to help them make connections between the ice cream they were making at school and the idea of an ice cream factory. She asked the children how they might find out how huge quantities of ice cream are made, and she wrote down what they said. Among their answers were:

- "Watch somebody do it."
- "Call the supermarket and ask them!"
- "Ask the cook."
- "Look on the Internet."
- "Go to Ben & Jerry's."

The teacher tried to follow up on the children's suggestions. They visited an ice cream and yogurt factory. They talked to other people and each other about ice cream. The body of information kept growing. Grandparents shared stories of eating ice cream all day when they got their tonsils out as children. The children wrote stories, drew pictures, collected recipes, went on field trips, and took photographs to document all this learning.

29

This class also had a make-your-own-sundae party. Families were invited. The children served the peach ice cream. The room was decorated with their charts, graphs, stories, drawings, and photographs. This party was a celebration of weeks of learning about something familiar to everyone. Meanwhile, the children were already talking about their next project for study: refrigeration! During the ice cream study, Emily's grandfather had told her about cutting ice from nearby lakes in winter to store and use for iceboxes in summer. Many of the children had never heard of pre-electricity refrigeration. They all swam in the lake where Emily's grandfather had cut ice in the "old days." They were fascinated by this story and curious about how food was kept fresh before electricity. Their learning was spiraling in new directions.

This story is an example of what Dewey would call an educational experience. The teacher observed and asked questions to find out what the children already knew. She set up experiences for them to discover things they didn't already know. She used her knowledge of child development to plan curriculum that was age appropriate, and she documented the children's learning to support her understanding of their thinking. The success of the project is measured by the fact that it led into the next area of study. The children were left curious, wanting more, and confident in their ability to dive in and satisfy their curiosity.

Dewey in the Twenty-First Century

A colleague with whom many of the ideas in this book were discussed for months prior to its publication used to have long talks with me about teaching. We both found ourselves concerned by the extent to which many of the teachers we spoke with had strong notions about paid planning time and articulated that when they left the building their job should be done until they return.

We talked about the hours of preparation we had always put in on nights and weekends when we were young teachers. We were researching community field trip ideas, going to the library for additional books to support the children's learning, looking in *National Geographic* and other magazines for photos that would authentically extend the subject matter we were involved in. It never occurred to us that when we walked out of our workplace our job was done. We are both passionate advocates of worthy wages for early childhood teachers and for expanded benefits and paid planning time. We are also educators who believe teaching is a passionate calling involving hours of preparation and planning that cannot possibly be fit into the workday.

In his book *My Pedagogic Creed*, Dewey references the need for teachers to teach children how to live in society. He believed that teachers shape society as well as individual children by what they do. A fine example of how this is currently being done is Head Start's I Am Moving, I Am Learning (IMIL) program. The program meets the individual as well as general needs of young children to learn conceptual information like colors, shapes, letters, and numbers in an active and fun way. At the same time, it addresses a serious societal problem in the United States: childhood obesity. It conveys the importance of good health to children by getting them up and moving and talking about the vegetables referenced in the songs, as well as how much fun it is to dance around to good music while helping their bodies to become strong and fit. An example of extending IMIL to other integrated approaches would be using the Early Sprouts approach by Karrie Kalich, Dottie Bauer, and Deirdre McPartlin for cooking and gardening experiences, also connected to taking good care of our bodies.

John Dewey supported parents at a time when the United States was transitioning from an agricultural to an industrial age. Had someone mentioned "going green" to Dewey, he would have thought we were referencing learning activities for children about color. But as we ponder his important theory about shaping society as we teach young children, we can apply this to the fact that we are transitioning again as a culture. The importance of teaching young children to care for the planet is not only interesting and relevant to the twenty-first century but also absolutely essential to our survival. Why not extend those Earth Day celebrations to include using the *Go Green Rating Scale* by Phil Boise. All of these programs are relatively new, yet each addresses the real-life issues that Dewey, Piaget, and Montessori repeatedly stressed as critically connected to educating the next generation.

For contemporary educators to learn from and utilize Dewey's theories of education, we must be willing to change with the times. When Dewey appealed to parents and teachers in his day to adapt to current societal changes rather than fight them, he was offering sound advice. It does not help to mourn the past or dread new trends that might make us uncomfortable.

In Scott Nearing's analysis of progressive education (2007), he refers to the school as a servant, not a master. He writes, "In that fact lies its greatness—the greatness of its opportunity and of its responsibility" (198). Nearing believes our responsibility is to be open to increased knowledge, which may prove more effective than the old theories we employ. At such times we need to embrace change. He cautions that this doesn't need to be done hastily but that change is inevitable.

For contemporary educators to learn from and utilize Dewey's theories of education, we must be willing to change with the times.

The early progressive educators frequently asked the question we continue to hear in current debates over school

32

directions: Does education exist for children, or do children exist for education? Today, as a century ago, this question is worthy of our discussion. Dewey's theory remains a clear guide to this debate.

Discussion Questions

1. Progressive education has been called many different things. What are some of the misconceptions about it? Give a brief explanation that summarizes Dewey's ideas about progressive education.

2. Today one common curriculum model is *emergent curriculum*, or planning curriculum around what *emerges* from the children's interests and experience. Is this consistent or inconsistent with Dewey's idea about education? Why?

3. Many families want an overtly structured environment for their children and feel anxious if they think that the children play too much. Using Dewey's ideas, prepare a response for families that illustrates the learning structure behind your program.

Suggestions for Further Reading

Dalton, Thomas C. 2002. *Becoming John Dewey: Dilemmas of a Philosopher and Naturalist*. Bloomington, IN: Indiana University Press.

Dewey, John, and Evelyn Dewey. 1915. *School of Tomorrow*. New York: E. P. Dutton.

Johnston, James Scott. 2006. *Inquiry and Education: John Dewey and The Quest for Democracy*. New York: State University of New York Press.

Chapter 2: Maria Montessori

The greatest sign of success for a teacher is to be able to say, "The children are now working as if I did not exist."

—Maria Montessori

Biography

MARIA MONTESSORI WAS BORN in Chiaravalle, Italy, in 1870. She was the only daughter of wealthy, well-educated parents. Her mother always encouraged her to think and study and pursue a professional career. Her father, a fairly conservative man, did not like having his daughter break with the traditional expectations for women of her era. He wanted his daughter to become a teacher, the only professional avenue considered appropriate to women at the time. However, he continued to support her when she became a student of science instead. She went on to medical school where she constantly struggled with the resentment of male medical students and her father's disapproval. As time went on, Montessori's scholarship earned the respect of her classmates. She specialized in pediatrics during her last two years, and in 1896 she became the first woman in Italy to graduate from medical school.

Montessori's first job was to visit insane asylums and select patients for treatment. This was where her interest in young children and their needs developed. She noticed that children who had been diagnosed as "unteachable" responded to her methods. Because she had trained as a scientist, she used observation to determine the needs of the children. She was a brilliant woman and an astute observer. Soon she determined that the problems existed not in the children, but in the adults, in their approaches and in the environments they provided. By this time, Montessori was developing a reputation for her gifts with children and education. She was referred to as "Teacher." Many forgot that her training was in medicine.

Montessori's first opportunity to work with typically developing children came in 1907, when she opened her first Casa dei Bambini (Children's House) in the slums of Rome. The building was offered to Montessori as an attempt to keep the children of working parents out of the streets. Shop owners thought it would reduce vandalism. Not only did the children come in from the streets but they became avid learners who loved to work and study. Montessori created a school environment to make up for the impoverished conditions of many of the children's homes. She determined that to be comfortable, young children need furnishings their own size and tools that fit their small hands. Because such things were not available at the time, Montessori made many of her own materials. She learned from her students. She wrote about her observations and theories and developed an international reputation for her work. By 1913 there were almost one hundred schools in the United States following Montessori's methods. In 1922 she was appointed a government inspector of schools in Italy. Her opposition to Mussolini's fascism forced her to leave the country in 1934.

Maria Montessori was nominated for the Nobel Peace Prize three times. When she died in Holland in 1952, she left educators of every nation a legacy of ideas and a collection of writings that still affect current practice in programs for young children. It is this legacy of ideas and how they affect our practices with children that provides the focus for this chapter.

Montessori's Theories

Many of Montessori's ideas are so basic to the ways we think about early childhood today that we take them for granted. Yet in 1907, when Dr. Montessori opened her first school, child-sized furnishings and tools and the idea of children working independently were considered radical. Her research into young children and what they need to learn has affected the fundamental ways early educators think about children. Her work provided a foundation for the work of such later theorists as Piaget and Vygotsky. Many of the ideas held by people who work in early childhood education today can be traced to Montessori.

In the United States, some early childhood programs call themselves Montessori programs. Because there are Montessori schools and Montessori materials, educators and others sometimes forget to separate Dr. Montessori's legacy of ideas about children and learning from specific Montessori programs. There is a wide range of diversity among these programs—some of them hold very firmly to Montessori principles, and some of them would never meet Montessori's own standards. It is important to understand that Montessori's theories about children have influenced the way all early childhood programs are struc-

Montessori's theories about children have influenced the way all early childhood programs are structured today.

tured today, not just programs that refer to themselves as Montessori programs. Her theories are important to early childhood teachers no matter what types of programs they work in.

37

Child-Centered Environments

Montessori acknowledged that the emphasis she placed on preparation of the learning environment was probably the main characteristic by which people identified her method. She believed that "environment" includes not only the space the children use and the furnishings and materials within that space but also the adults and the children who share their days with each other, as well as the outdoor environment and other places where children learn. Montessori believed that children learn language and other significant life skills without conscious effort from the environments where they spend their time. For that reason, she thought that environments for children need to be beautiful and orderly so that children can learn order from them. She believed children learn best through sensory experiences. She thought that the teacher has a responsibility to provide wonderful sights, textures, sounds, and smells for children. She also believed that part of sensory experience for children is having tools and utensils that fit their small hands and tables and chairs that match their small bodies. Beautiful, orderly, child-sized environments and sensory play are part of Montessori's legacy.

Most American early childhood programs have child-sized furnishings, equipment, and utensils. What else can teachers learn from Montessori's understanding of good environments for children? Montessori thought that early childhood teachers should

- provide real tools that work, such as sharp knives, good scissors, and woodworking and cleaning tools;

- keep materials and equipment accessible to the children and organized so they can find and put away what they need; and

- create beauty and order in the classroom.

38

Provide Real Tools That Work
Montessori suggested that the size of furnishings and materials is important. When she opened her schools in Italy, child-sized tools and furnishings were not available. This was why she became so involved in making her own materials. Montessori took this part of environment planning so seriously that even the staircase in her school was custom-designed to fit her students' small feet. When we see classrooms outfitted with child-sized hammers, saws, and workbenches, we are looking at Montessori's influence. Child-sized pitchers for pouring juice and small mixing bowls and pots also demonstrate her influence.

The fact that these child-sized tools really work is also part of Montessori's educational philosophy. She thought children needed real tools if they were to do the real work that interested them. In our preschools, children are often expected to cut paper with scissors that aren't sharp or cut vegetables with butter knives so they won't be hurt. Unfortunately, these dull tools also make these simple tasks very difficult, and in some cases, more dangerous than if children used sharp tools properly. Montessori believed that children could learn to use tools safely, and that giving them tools that didn't really work undermined their competence.

Keep Materials and Equipment Accessible to the Children
In addition to having real tools, Montessori stressed the need for children to be able to reach materials when they needed them in order to help children become responsible for their own learning. Arranging classrooms with low, open shelves means children can see what is available and get what they want without assistance from the teacher. They should not have to interrupt their work to get the attention of the busy teacher or ask permission to use the materials they need.

Often in our preschools, supplies are kept out of the children's reach. For example, teachers plan an art activity and "get the paint out" instead of having paint available all the time for children to use. Teachers following Montessori's lead have ample supplies available for children to access and use. With help from the children, they keep these supplies well organized so that choices and opportunities continually invite the children to be creative.

Often when teachers hesitate to arrange materials in an accessible way, they say it is because the children would make too much mess. Montessori made it clear that it is a serious teaching responsibility to become "the keeper and custodian of the environment" ([1949] 1967, 277). She believed that the teacher should prepare a clean, organized, and orderly environment for the children. If every material has a place that is clearly marked in a child-friendly way, with photographs or drawings as well as the printed name of the material that belongs there, children have the power to get what they need and also to put it away when they are done.

Create Beauty and Order

Montessori used the word *cheerful* to describe well-planned spaces for children. She believed caring for the environment and keeping it bright and orderly should be viewed as a teaching skill. Too often, teachers view cleaning and organizing as additional work not in their job description. According to Montessori, knowing how to arrange an interesting, beautiful environment for children is as much a part of teaching as knowing how to select fine children's books for the library. Montessori said, "Our apparatus for educating

According to Montessori, knowing how to arrange an interesting, beautiful environment for children is as much a part of teaching as knowing how to select fine children's books for the library.

40

the senses offers the child a key to guide his exploration of the world" ([1949] 1967, 183).

Teachers need to ask themselves what they are providing in the environment to "educate the senses." What sights and sounds do children hear when they enter the room? What is available to touch or taste? What music is playing and when? Are lilacs brought in when they are in bloom? Are windows opened to let the fresh air in? Does soft lamp light offer a break from the constant glare and hum of fluorescent lights? Are the displays of children's art carefully hung? Is there a color scheme in the room, or does the purple shelf Josh's family donated sit next to the blue shelves that the toddler teachers didn't want anymore? Were fund-raising monies used to buy a lovely and comfortable new sofa, or is the sofa one that was donated because the springs stick through the dirty, dated upholstery and no adult would sit on it?

Adults sometimes act as if children have no interest in the beauty of their surroundings. There is an encouraged stereotype that children like to "mess up" but not "clean up." Observations of young children do not bear this out. Montessori believed that beauty and order are critical to pre-pared environments for children. That message is echoed today in the work of educators inspired by the teachers of Reggio Emilia, Italy.

For example, if a child's art is matted on colored paper that brings out the child's choice of colors for his painting, and if it is hung in a special display area, the children will learn to appreciate color and design. Another example is bringing in fresh flowers to grace the lunch table or the top of the book-case. Walking in a field to pick flowers to make the classroom lovely is a fine way to spend a morning.

One Head Start teacher I know hangs a famous still life painting in her studio area each week. (A *still life* is an arrangement of flowers or vegetables or small household items.) She sets up her own similar still life nearby. Some children try to draw it. Some children talk about the items included in it. Others don't seem to notice, yet its presence communicates respect for beauty as part of the children's day.

Competence and Responsibility

Montessori believed that children want and need to care for themselves and their surroundings. She believed that adults spent too much time "serving" children. She cautioned teachers to remember that children who are not allowed to do something for themselves do not learn how to do it. Montessori understood that it is sometimes much easier to do something for children than it is to take the time and energy to teach them to do it for themselves. But she also believed that for children to grow and develop skills, the adults in their lives need to make opportunities for children to do things for themselves. Fostering independence is part of Montessori's legacy.

Montessori believed that children learn best by doing and through repetition. She thought they do things over and over to make an experience their own, as well as to develop skills. Montessori urged teachers not to interfere with the child's patterns and pace of learning. She thought it is the teacher's job to prepare the environment, provide appropriate materials, and then step back and allow the children the time and space to experiment. Open-ended scheduling, with large blocks of time for free work and play, is part of Montessori's legacy.

How can early childhood teachers apply Montessori's thinking about competence and responsibility in their programs? Montessori thought teachers should give children responsibility for keeping the community space clean and orderly. She also thought teachers should provide large blocks of time for free work and play and allow children to structure their own time.

Allow Children to Take Responsibility

Montessori was convinced that the more teachers manage for children, the harder the job will be. Children have a passionate interest in real work. They love to watch the cook, the custodian, and the garbage collectors at work. They always want to "help." Montessori believed that children should be able to do everything they are capable of. She believed it is the teacher's responsibility to increase each child's competence whenever possible.

Frequently, early childhood teachers feel frustration that they are unable to do as much cleaning and organizing in their rooms as necessary. They feel frustrated and overwhelmed when the Legos, Unifix cubes, and pattern blocks get all mixed up and out of place. Many teachers plan sorting activities but never think to give the children the task of sorting materials into their proper places in the classroom. Teachers know that water play is calming for children, yet they worry about making time to clean because they are too busy planning activities for the water table! If children were given warm, soapy water and scrub brushes, they could clean the tables and chairs themselves. Montessori claimed that the sense of competence children gain from involvement in such real-life work is extremely beneficial and enhances the child's self-esteem in a way that artificial or contrived activities never could.

Schedule Large Blocks of Open-Ended Time

Montessori's observations led her to believe that children are capable of great concentration when they are surrounded by many interesting things to do and given the time and freedom to do them. She thought that as teachers allow children to choose what they will do and how and when they will do it, the teachers have more time to observe and assist children individually. Today in our early childhood programs, children are often called to circle or story time when they are deeply engaged in a project of their own. Teachers say they have so much to teach the children in a short amount of time that they are unable to leave the children to their own interests as much as they would like. Some teachers feel that they aren't teaching unless they have planned all the activities. They use plan books in which blocks of time are reserved for writing, stories and music, manipulatives, math games, and snack. Many teachers are afraid to set plan books aside. They may even call reluctant children inside on a beautiful, sunny day because an activity, such as "movement with silk scarves," is on the schedule.

Montessori teachers, on the other hand, are trained to teach little and observe much. Teachers, of course, must plan activities and have materials on hand to support the children's interests, as suggested by Dewey's ideas in chapter 1. However, it is important to recognize the difference between the kind of aimless activity Dewey spoke out against and purposeful, self-directed activity. When children are engaged in serious work and learning, they are not as likely to be disruptive. Montessori's theory about young children tells teachers not to pull children away from projects that interest them unless it's absolutely necessary.

Montessori believed that the only way to know how to schedule the day and manage behavior is through observation. This is also why large blocks of uninterrupted time are so important to both teachers and children in early childhood classrooms. Teachers too often think they don't need to be involved during this time. The time, however, allows the perfect opportunity for teachers to observe both the quality of the group play as well as an individual child's participation in that group play. An example of the difference observation can make to scheduling can be drawn from looking at two teachers working in the same kindergarten program but in separate classrooms.

Janet believes that keeping consistent schedules is important for the children. Every weekend she plans carefully for the coming week. She tries to balance indoor with outdoor time, active with quiet activities, and child-choice with teacher-directed activities. She keeps individual needs in mind. Once the plan is established, she is hesitant to change it. She believes the children are calmed by their consistent routines.

Down the hall, Bonnie agrees with Janet philosophically about what is important for young children. She admits, however, that she doesn't spend as much time planning as Janet does. She relies more heavily on constant, ongoing observation of the kindergarten children. Bonnie claims she wouldn't know how to pace her days without carefully watching the children for signs of interest, fatigue, and needs.

The difference between these two teachers becomes even more pronounced when examining how they manage one simple part of their day: outdoor time. Janet frequently struggles with it. She and her assistant, Laura, find that five or six of their class of eighteen are always too cold or too hot or otherwise unhappy about being outdoors. The two teachers' ability to focus on the children who are invigorated by being outdoors is diminished by the energy spent keeping the five or six stragglers from mutiny. Once they are indoors again, Janet's and Laura's energy is consumed by trying to reel in the children who need a longer period of outdoor play.

Bonnie and her assistant, Mark, have found an easier way. When possible, they offer children choices about how long they spend outdoors. When Bonnie and Mark observe that five or six children are getting tired, one of them takes the small group indoors. Their careful observation and flexibility allows both scheduling and behavior management to go more smoothly.

Observation

Since Montessori trained as a doctor, she brought the skills of a scientist to the classroom. When she turned her energies toward the education of young children, it seemed only natural to use her scientific skills. She believed that if you are going to teach, you need to know all you can about those you hope to educate. She believed that the way to get to know children is to watch them. Careful observation, to Montessori, is the key to determining what the children are interested in or need to learn. She believed every child could learn. She was convinced that if children are not learning, adults are not listening carefully enough or watching closely enough. Careful observation is part of her legacy. Take time for careful observation and reflection, and use these observations to guide your environment and curriculum planning.

She believed every child could learn. She was convinced that if children are not learning, adults are not listening carefully enough or watching closely enough.

Many early childhood programs don't take time for careful observation and reflection. "We are too busy," some teachers say. Yet in the same conversation one might hear, "What can we do about these kids? They don't listen. They don't focus. There is too much running around and hitting in this classroom. How can I do observations when these kids have such demanding needs? I can't fit it in!" Montessori suggested that if we watch children carefully and then reflect on those observations, we can figure out what the children need that they are not presently getting from the environment.

For example, I remember observing in a classroom where children's physical aggression was taking much of the teachers' time. I noticed that they were using a wonderful woodworking bench as a science table. "Do you have tools?" I asked.

46

Both teachers rolled their eyes and said, "Look around this room. These children don't go five minutes without hurting each other. Are you suggesting we should hand an already out-of-control group of children a bunch of hammers? Then we would really have problems!"

I asked why they thought the children acted this way. The teachers said they thought the children were not interested in doing any activities.

"Are there times when they are not as aggressive?" I asked. The answer won't surprise you. The teachers said that when they walked to the park, the children were able to run and climb and did not use their physical energy on each other. I asked if the teachers would be willing to try putting out the tools to see what would happen. They agreed.

Both teachers were surprised at the outcome. The children became very involved with the hammers and nails. The children started hammering just for the sake of pounding nails, and they stopped hitting each other. The teachers had a little respite and were able to talk with each other about how to do more with the children's obvious need for physical release. Montessori viewed observation in this way as a jumping-off point that helped teachers know what children needed and wanted to be doing.

The teachers described above learned something new from their observations: the children needed more physical activity. They also learned that the activities offered previously had not captivated the children. The high energy level and the lack of solid curriculum to engage that energy had resulted in challenging behavior. After considerable discussion and reflection on these observations, the teachers decided that they needed to change the physical environment as well as the curriculum. They put some furnishings in storage and provided more space for gross-motor activities. They went to a workshop on movement and started experimenting more creatively with different kinds of music in the classroom. They increased the use of jazz and rock for children's dance experiences. The more the children moved, the less inappropriate physical aggression occurred.

Initially, these teachers were not convinced of Montessori's premise that observing children will give teachers clues to their curriculum needs. They were working hard to provide appropriate activities and experiences, but the ideas were coming from curriculum manuals, not from the children. Allowing children to provide the ideas for curriculum made their classroom a more peaceful and also a more exciting place to be.

Montessori in the Twenty-First Century

The teachers described above were struggling to meet the needs of young children to move and get physical activity. They learned that observing can teach us a great deal about what the children need. Unfortunately, after all the progress made in the United States in terms of developmentally appropriate practices, many early educators report that in their post–No Child Left Behind preschool and kindergarten classrooms they no longer have time or "permission" to allow children to play or pursue their own interests. Some kindergarten children no longer have outdoor playtime. There are times when we can easily get discouraged and feel that trends are moving backward, not progressing. This is a time, once again, when knowing the theoretical foundations of our discipline well is essential. It is essential so we can give good reasons *why* we do what we do with children when challenged by well-intentioned parents, administrators, or school board members.

It is clear that Montessori had strong feelings about the tendency of adults to undermine children's competence by doing too much for them. She used the word *serving* in her discussions and cautioned teachers that children remain incompetent if adults do for them what they are capable of doing themselves. Today we see a frightening return to this kind of thinking. Teachers frequently complain to me of parents who carry their five-year-olds because they are in a hurry. We often see overwhelmed and tired parents at the end of the day who are trying to carry not only their child but also the child's lunch box, backpack, and teddy bear out to the car, rather than asking the five-year-old to walk and carry half of the equipment. Walking is a basic skill for most of us, but this is a good example of a twenty-first-century tendency to spare children (usually middle-class children) any effort, inconvenience, or stress. Polly Young-Eisendrath, in her 2008 book, *The Self-Esteem Trap: Raising Confident and Compassionate Kids in an Age of Self-Importance,* echoes Montessori's concerns of a century ago: she describes the parents who are serving their children in a way that is detrimental to their children's growth and development.

Another contemporary writer, Diana West, goes so far as to warn that this tendency is a threat to western civilization. Her book *The Death of the Grown-Up: How America's Arrested Development Is Bringing Down Western Civilization* is a "must read" for today's concerned parents and teachers. She describes the ways in which many thirty-year-olds in the United States are still functional adolescents. It is a frightening trend. Just as a century ago when Montessori urged teachers to organize environments for children and then make the time for children to manage on their own, young children today need teachers who will heed this warning and stand up for children's rights to do all that they are capable of doing. This does not mean we can't tie shoes or help with a jacket when a child is

Young children today need teachers who will heed this warning and stand up for children's rights to do all that they are capable of doing.

49

tired or irritable just because we know she can do it herself. But it does mean that there is a well-documented trend, once again, to deprive children of the satisfaction and competence that independence nurtures. Montessori's legacy is as important today as it was when she first shared her brilliant understanding of the needs of young children.

Discussion Questions

1. Last week you had a big cleaning day in your program. The children took their chairs and toys outside and scrubbed them down with soapy water and brushes. Today a dad came in with a complaint that he does not pay tuition for his children to do your cleaning. Basing your response on Montessori's ideas about real jobs and responsibility, what would you say?

2. How would you use Montessori's ideas to approach the idea of early literacy in preschool programs? What kinds of materials and equipment would you use in the classroom, and what kinds of activities would you plan? Describe how Montessori's theory supports your plan.

3. Your coteacher has complained that plants take up too much space in the classroom and create additional work. You suggest that the children take over all responsibility for the plants. He complains that they don't have enough time now and that would be wasting their valuable time. Using Montessori's ideas on independence and environment, how could you convince your coteacher that this is a good investment of the children's time?

Suggestions for Further Reading

Hainstock, Elizabeth G. 1997. *The Essential Montessori: An Introduction to the Woman, the Writings, the Method, and the Movement.* New York: Plume.

Lillard, Angeline Stoll. 2005. *Montessori: The Science behind the Genius.* New York: Oxford University Press.

Montessori, Maria. 1965. *Dr. Montessori's Own Handbook: A Short Guide to Her Ideas and Materials.* New York: Schocken Books.

Chapter 3: Erik Erikson

There is in every child at every stage a new miracle of vigorous unfolding, which constitutes a new hope and a new responsibility for all.

—Erik Erikson

Biography

ERIK ERIKSON WAS BORN in Frankfurt, Germany, in 1902. He was an artist and teacher who became interested in psychology when he met Anna Freud. Freud was a psychoanalyst and the daughter of Sigmund Freud. She convinced Erikson to study at the Vienna Psychoanalytic Institute, where he specialized in child psychoanalysis.

He came to the United States in 1933, where he joined the faculty of Harvard Medical School. Later he moved to Yale University, where he became interested in the influence of culture and society on child development. His first book, *Childhood and Society*, originally published in 1950, is considered a classic by educators, psychologists, and sociologists.

Erikson's later years were devoted to exploring the ways adults can continue to live meaningful and productive lives in their old age. He continued to work on development issues until he died at the age of ninety-two in 1994.

Erikson's Theories

Erikson's work has importance for every early childhood educator because it shows how children develop the foundation for emotional and social development and mental health. Erikson's theory of psychosocial development, which is called the *Eight Ages of Man*, covers the entire life span of a human being. It is Erikson's idea that there is a task that must be accomplished at each stage of development. Successful resolution of each stage affects the next stage. As people pass through each stage, they form personality strengths or weaknesses based on their development during that stage. Describing this, Erikson gave us the term *identity crisis*. He considered it inevitable that young people experience conflict as they grow and change into adults.

The following chart illustrates each of the eight ages Erickson identified, names each one as a stage, and lists its

Erikson's Stages of Psychosocial Development		
Age	**Stage**	**Strength Developed**
Birth to 12 months	Trust vs. Mistrust	Hope
1–3 years	Autonomy vs. Shame and Doubt	Willpower
3–6 years	Initiative vs. Guilt	Purpose
6–11 years	Industry vs. Inferiority	Competence
Adolescence	Identity vs. Role Confusion	Fidelity
Young adulthood	Intimacy vs. Isolation	Love
Middle age	Generativity vs. Self-Absorption	Care
Old age	Integrity vs. Despair	Wisdom

(Erikson [1950] 1963)

strength, which is also the ideal result of the developmental struggle concluded at that stage. In *Childhood and Society*, Erikson also discusses the weaknesses resulting from failure to resolve each struggle. These are discussed in the rest of this chapter.

Erikson was convinced that in the earliest years of life, patterns develop that regulate, or at least influence, a person's actions and interactions for the rest of his or her life. However, he also wrote, "There are, therefore . . . few frustrations in either this or the following stages which the growing child cannot endure if the frustration leads to the ever-renewed experience of greater sameness and stronger continuity of development, toward a final integration of the individual life cycle with some meaningful wider belongingness" (Erikson [1950] 1963, 249). He believed it was always possible to go back and renegotiate issues from a previous stage of development. He was convinced that the tasks of each stage continue to present themselves at times of crisis in love and work throughout our lives. Though it is true that basic trust and independence are formed early and affect later actions and attributes, it is also true that people can choose to work toward a better resolution of any of these developmental tasks at any time throughout their lives. Erikson felt that the early childhood years were critical in children's development of trust, *autonomy*, and initiative, but he did not believe all was lost if children experienced difficulties in the first three stages.

We can refer to these three stages as "windows of opportunity," or developmental timetables. They signify when the brain is most fertile for taking in specific types of learning. For example, the window of opportunity for Erikson's trust vs. mistrust stage is associated with the first twelve months of life. Experiences that occur within these twelve months help to determine whether a baby will "wire" for trust or mistrust. If a baby's needs are regularly met, the baby will wire for trust. However, if a baby's needs are not regularly met, the baby is likely to wire for mistrust. And, the further a baby grows from the window of opportunity, the more difficult the repair. But repair is still possible with the right interactions and environment. In the article "Linking Brain Principles to High-Quality Early Childhood Education" from the November–December 2011 issue of *Exchange* magazine, authors Stephen Rushton and Anne Juola-Rushton write:

> *Neuroscientists now understand that the brain's neurons continue to both develop (plasticity) and disappear (pruning) throughout most of our lives. However, we experience the greatest growth—and a high volume of pruning—in early childhood. . . . This process slows down somewhat after birth. However, up until the age of 12, pathways continue to be formed and . . . develop as the child interacts with her environment. Those neurons that are not stimulated or make connections to other neurons are pruned away and dissolve. . . . Providing meaningful, positive experiences for children actually alters the formation of their brains! (9)*

Erikson's first three stages are discussed here since these are the stages that affect children in the early childhood years.

Trust vs. Mistrust

Erikson's first stage of psychosocial development, which takes place during the first year of life, is trust versus mistrust. Babies' task during this time is to develop a sense of trust in themselves, in other people, and in the world around them. Erikson wrote about trust as having two parts, *external*—belief that significant adults will be present to meet the baby's needs—and *internal*—belief in her own power to effect change and cope with a variety of circumstances. Babies

56

who successfully adapt during this first stage approach their second year of life with a sure sense that the world is a good place to be. They believe that adults will be there to meet their physical needs and to guide and support them. They trust that adults will lend stability and continuity of care to their lives. They know they have the power to engage adults through tears, smiles, or fussing whenever they need an adult's help.

This engaging of adults is part of what we call *attachment*. It is a special bond between babies and the significant adults in their lives. When a securely attached baby is in the presence of these adults, her sense of security and comfort is heightened. The baby uses the adults as a safe place from which to go out and explore the world. When she encounters a threat of any kind, such as unusual sights, sounds, or situations, she needs to be able to return quickly to the arms of a trusted adult for comfort and reassurance. When babies develop a strong sense of trust during their first year, they become attached to the important people in their lives.

Erikson believed that accomplishment of each developmental stage lays the foundation for the next stage. A basic sense of trust is necessary for children to move into the next stage and develop autonomy. For example, a common characteristic of children who lack strong attachments with important adults is the failure to develop *empathy* (the ability to put yourself in another person's place and understand how she feels). In recent years when juveniles have committed violent crimes and expressed no remorse, headlines have asked, "Why?" The answer, of course, is far more complex than Erikson's theory of psychosocial development. Yet some of his writing of a half century ago seems prophetic in light of the state of many children today. When children's needs go unmet, they are unable to develop trust in themselves or the world around them. According to Erikson, children lacking this basic sense of trust are incapable of developing higher levels of social functioning.

Erikson believed that two actions on the part of parents and teachers help babies develop this basic sense of trust: holding babies close and having warm physical contact with them when they are being fed and responding right away to their distress when they cry or fuss. Both of these actions are critical teaching skills for infant care providers. Increasing numbers of very young babies are spending their days in child care centers or in family child care. Changing social conditions do not change the developmental needs of young children. The needs of babies for predictable, loving care have not changed. Our challenge, then, is to create places where babies' needs are met and where parents' attempts to meet their babies' needs are received with a joyful, welcoming response by teachers. Child care centers must provide an atmosphere in which babies, and their families, can thrive. These next actions are three important aspects of supporting the development of trust. I write in-depth on them in my book *Theories of Attachment*.

Teachers wanting to support the development of trust in infants need to

- hold babies during feedings,

- respond to signals of distress, and

- support babies' attachment through primary caregiving.

Hold Babies During Feedings

The pleasure of warmth and cuddling when babies are being fed is as essential an ingredient for emotional development as the nutritious meal is for physical development. At this early age it is through their feelings that babies learn. When a familiar adult's smiling face kisses and cuddles a baby at feeding time, she learns that she is important and lovable. Once teachers know that comfort and pleasure for infants during feeding is as important as the nutrition, they can plan the program in the infant room to allow for these. Soft lights, calming music, and a rocking chair set the stage for pleasant mealtimes. The importance of building relationships during feedings requires that teachers focus on the baby—smiling, cuddling, and talking.

The importance of building relationships during feedings requires that teachers focus on the baby—smiling, cuddling, and talking.

This isn't a time for teachers to talk with each other about next week's staff meeting! Some centers post signs on the door to the infant room stating, "No interruptions, please. We are having lunch!" This gives the clear message that phone calls, messages, and visitors (except, of course, the babies' parents) are not welcome during this special time for teachers and babies.

Since attachment to special adults is an important piece of this stage of development, arranging for the same teacher to feed the same babies as much as schedules can possibly allow supports the babies in their acquisition of that basic sense of trust.

Erikson makes it clear that a huge piece of accomplishing this first stage of development is the quality of the parent-child relationship. Babies need as much warm, loving contact with their parents as they can get. For this reason, infant programs must provide not only a welcoming attitude toward nursing mothers but also a physical space offering privacy, quiet music, and comfortable seating where mothers and babies can share a special mealtime. And, for nursing mothers who aren't able to breast-feed during the day, the program needs to accept pumped breast milk for bottle feedings.

Respond to Distress

In every child development course I've ever taught, someone has asked about "spoiling" children by responding to them when they cry. Once an infant teacher rolled her eyes at me as she walked with a screaming baby and said, "This child is just too attached to her parents! I'm trying to teach her that we can't just come running every time she cries!"

If teachers provide care based on Erikson's theories, they accept that babies have few coping skills and that it is therefore up to adults to keep them comfortable. Programs whose staff understand infant development have policies of quickly responding to babies' tears. In the United States, though, the notion persists that adults "spoil" babies by giving them the attention they cry for.

On the flip side, some parents never give their children the opportunity to cope with any level of distress. Current studies (Young-Eisendrath 2008) as well as Montessori's original work on developing independence and Magda Gerber's 1997 (among her other) work on competence have all stressed the importance of learning to cope. Babies whose needs are consistently met quickly can learn to cope with small amounts of distress. Parents and teachers need the confidence to let them try to cope in small doses. It's a matter of balance.

Erikson's theory says that babies will develop the strongest sense of security if they know that adults will come running when they cry. Then, when they are a little older, they will be able to cope with delayed gratification of their needs. By meeting their needs quickly and consistently throughout their first year of life, adults are doing the opposite of spoiling. With consistent, responsive care, they are laying the foundation that will allow babies to grow into strong, confident toddlers ready to assert their independence.

Support Attachment through Primary Caregiving

Erikson's theory of infant development assures teachers and parents that it is impossible for babies under a year of age to be "too attached" to the special adults in their lives. The teacher in the story above who wanted to teach the baby that adults can't always be there was missing the central point of providing quality care to infants. Attachment is what developing a sense of trust is all about. It is the teacher's job to provide as much stability of care as possible. For this reason, organizing staff schedules in an infant program around primary caregivers is a good idea.

Erikson stressed how important it is for babies to have significant relationships with a few key adults in order to accomplish the task of developing basic trust. For these relationships to develop in child care settings, babies need to count on the same adult being there when they wake from a nap, need their diaper changed, come in from a walk, or need to be fed. Both parents and teachers sometimes raise objections to primary caregiving. Some teachers in infant care settings say that babies cry all day if their primary caregiver is absent from the center. Parents, too, will sometimes say, "I worry that she is too attached to her primary caregiver. Last week when the teacher was out sick, my baby cried all day."

Like the old adage "It's better to have loved and lost than never to have loved at all," Erikson's theory confirms that strong relationships with a few significant adults in the first year of life are important, even if the babies have to separate later from the people to whom they are attached. The fact that separation from those special adults causes distress for babies and demands the comfort of others is not a good reason, according to Erikson, to try to prevent this attachment. Attachment is essential, even if it is not permanent, and the process of mourning for a special adult and being comforted by other reliable adults is another indication to babies that their needs will be met.

Autonomy versus Shame and Doubt

Erikson's second stage of psychosocial development, which takes place during the second and third year of life, is *autonomy versus shame and doubt.* The developmental task of this stage is to acquire a sense of autonomy (independence) without suffering extremes of shame and doubt. Children who successfully adapt during this stage of development will acquire a strong sense of self. They will be able to separate confidently, for limited periods of time, from parents and primary caregivers. They will demand that they do things for themselves whenever possible. Toddler teachers become accustomed to hearing, "No! Me! Mine! Me do it!" which are characteristic of this stage of development. Toddlers also have a way of being fiercely independent one minute and needy and clingy the next.

According to Erikson, this is all a natural part of toddler development. He said that children during this second stage are dealing with the challenges of holding on and letting go. Erikson meant several things by this. He knew that both holding on and letting go can be positive and negative forces in human behavior. Holding on can be destructive: controlling, unyielding, and uncooperative behaviors. Holding on can also be constructive: attachment to special people, courage in the face of adversity, or plain old persistence in getting a task done. Letting go can be destructive: tantrums, losing control when angry, hitting, or biting. Letting go can also be constructive: cooperating in relationships, sharing,

Children, during this second stage, are dealing with the challenges of holding on and letting go.

or yielding to the plans of others. Again, it is a matter of balance.

Erikson believed that toddlers struggle to achieve balance between appropriate holding on and letting go. Areas for these struggles include sharing with friends, relationships with parents and primary caregivers, independent toileting, and making choices. Erikson thought that one of the main barriers for toddlers in accomplishing this task is overcontrolling behavior from adults who thwart and resist the toddlers' growing demands for independence. When adults are unable to adjust to a child's swinging between needs for dependence and independence at this stage, they often shame the child for behavior that is actually developmentally appropriate. For children, the effects of this shaming response are twofold. In the short term, the toddler becomes even more frustrated and resistive. In the long term, the child models the adult behavior, becoming controlling and unyielding herself. In order to develop a strong sense of independence, toddlers need to have reasonable opportunities for choice and control. At the same time, they need consistent, firm, reassuring limits set by caring adults. Toddlers can easily be victims of their own strong feelings and sometimes do need adults to step in. It is our responsibility to do so.

Erikson said that this stage is an important time in development because its outcomes determine, to a great extent, the ratio of love and hate, cooperation or lack of it, and freedom of expression or tendency to suppress feelings that become part of who children are for the rest of their lives. When children can fully develop a strong sense of self-control without loss of self-esteem, they will feel proud and confident. But when children experience loss of control and excessive shame, they will tend to doubt themselves. Again, in light of the more current studies cited above, adequate, not excessive, self-esteem is our goal for positive emotional health.

It is clear that adults who care for toddlers have a balancing act on their hands as they guide them throughout this tumultuous stage. Erikson believed that, with the support and understanding of significant adults, toddlers can navigate this stage, emerging confident and ready to take the initiative in their next stage of development. Erikson believed that adults can foster independence in children of this age by

- giving children simple choices;

- not giving false choices;

- setting clear, consistent, reasonable limits; and

- accepting children's swings between independence and dependence, and reassuring them that both are okay.

Erikson believed that children need to be able to experience the fury and demands of this unpredictable stage of their development without losing the support and reassurance of the important adults in their lives. If adults provide choices and clear limits at this stage, a toddler can thrive and feel comfortable with his need to be a "big boy" one minute and a "baby" the next.

How can toddlers' teachers apply Erikson's theory?

- Give children simple choices.

- Eliminate false choices.

- Set clear limits for children.

- Accept alternating needs for independence and dependence.

Give Children Simple Choices

According to Erikson, toddlers need to experience the independence of being able to make some choices for themselves. Toddler programs can support their independence by arranging for self-selection of activities and materials. Rooms should include low shelves for equipment where toddlers can make

64

their choices without help from others. There should be duplicates or multiple copies of favorite toys and books since sharing is not yet a well-developed skill. This makes life easier for teachers and happier for toddlers since it reduces territorial toddler conflict.

Schedules should include lots of time in which toddlers can choose what they want to do from a range of acceptable options. Teachers should avoid expecting all the children to do the same thing at the same time. Teachers can support toddlers in making reasonable choices for themselves and expressing their preferences, even when it's not possible to do exactly what the children would like to do at that moment. Teachers can acknowledge toddlers' feelings with phrases such as, "I know you want to go outside right now. I wish we could go out, too. We can go out when all the diapers are changed."

Choices need to be simple at this age to help children learn how to choose and to keep the alternatives manageable for teachers. Most two-year-olds aren't ready for "What would you like for lunch today?" But choosing between a cheese sandwich and a peanut butter sandwich offers just the right challenge. Looking at a drawer full of clothing might reduce a toddler to tears or a tantrum because the choices are so overwhelming. Choosing between a red shirt and a yellow shirt offers a toddler enough independence to feel she has control over her life.

Eliminate False Choices

Many teachers make the mistake of offering toddlers a choice when there really isn't one. It's very confusing for children who are trying to learn how much control they really have to be asked a rhetorical question. Adults and school-age children can understand that "Would you like to do the dishes?" is a request or the polite phrasing of an expectation. Toddlers cannot distinguish between this kind of question and a real choice. For this reason, teachers are sometimes surprised when they ask, "Would you like to go out to play now?" and the child who thought she had a choice wails at being thrust into her jacket against her will.

To offer children in this stage the control they need, try phrasing necessary changes in a way that offers a choice of *how* (not *whether*) the task will be accomplished. For example, state, "We are going out now. Would you like me to help you put on your jacket, or do you want to do it yourself?" This makes it clear that the doing (going out, coming in, taking a nap, and so on) is not a choice. The choice is whether the child gets ready by himself or receives some adult help.

Set Clear Limits

Erikson believed that the child's struggles between inner and outer control are great at this age. Toddlers are working on their sense of self. Their sense of others is still primitive. They will push, hit, bite, and throw things in a most matter-of-fact way. For this reason, teachers do children a service during this stage when they don't shy away from clear, firm limits. When outer limits—those imposed by adults—are clear, children can focus on learning inner control. When outer limits are inconsistent or poorly stated, children continually have to put energy into finding out what they are.

This is an area where I have observed less teacher competence in the new millennium than previously. As stated in the last paragraph, stating limits clearly is essential to helping toddlers meet their own needs. Working on teacher talk that is not confusing will help teachers with this stage. This topic is discussed at length in my book *Use Your Words*.

Accept Alternating Needs for Independence and Dependence

When toddlers strive for independence, they do it with passion. Their insistence on having things their way can be

66

downright defiant! According to Erikson, it is critical to healthy development for children to have their own way at this stage. Unless a child is putting herself or someone else in danger, toddler teachers need to support the child's drive to do something her own way. Teachers should yield to children's need to be held and rocked and also to their fierce need to do things for themselves. When teachers understand that this seesaw behavior is a normal part of toddler development, it is easier to cope with the variety of moods and behaviors a toddler will present in a short period of time. Teachers' acceptance of these changing moods helps toddlers to grow in confidence and self-esteem.

Again, the culture in the United States today calls for some adaptation to our approach to toddler tantrums. It is probably fair to say that decades ago, both parents and teachers were not tolerant enough, but today's parents and teachers are at risk of tolerating too much.

Toddlers' constantly changing needs for dependence and independence can be supported in the environment as well. Easels, water tables, and dramatic play materials are as important to toddlers as they are to preschoolers. Soft toys, board books, and push/pull toys are as important here as in environments for younger babies. This approach to environment offers comfort to children as they engage alternately in "big kid" and "baby" behaviors throughout their toddler days.

Initiative versus Guilt

The third and last stage of Erikson's theory that addresses the early childhood years is *initiative versus guilt.* Most four- and five-year-olds are at this stage, which is therefore a key one for preschool and kindergarten teachers to know about. The developmental task of this stage is to acquire a sense of purpose.

Erikson describes children of this age as energetic and ready to learn. Typically developing children will forget failures more quickly by four or five. They are more willing to listen and learn from teachers, parents, and other children. At this stage children are growing in ways that make them much more actively focused and less defiant. Children who have negotiated their second stage successfully have established their autonomy, so they act less for the sake of individual control and more to get things done. Children who successfully accomplish the developmental tasks of this stage will emerge confident and competent. They will believe that they can plan and complete a task independently. They will be able to cope with and learn from mistakes without feeling guilty for things that don't go as planned.

At first glance, this stage seems much easier for adults caring for children than the previous two. Part of that has to do with children's growing cognitive and physical abilities. The developmental task also does not require as much energy from adults. In addition, it involves less of the aggressive behavior that is so much a part of toddler development. According to Erikson, however, it is a time when the child's development can split in one of two possible directions: human potential for glory or for destruction. If we encourage preschool children to use their energy in an active and involved way, their confidence will grow. Their competence will increase. If we do for them what they can do for themselves or if we focus on the mistakes they make on the way to developing new skills, their sense of initiative can turn to guilt and discouragement. Again, just as we revisited the concept of developing independence in the last chapter, it is critical to do so

If we encourage preschool children to use their energy in an active and involved way, their confidence will grow. Their competence will increase.

68

here as well. There seems to be less tendency today to focus on children's mistakes in a negative way. However (as previously stated and cited), there is a documented trend of parents consistently doing for children what they are capable of doing themselves.

Of course, most teachers don't purposefully focus on children's mistakes instead of on their successes. However, according to Erikson, when teachers hover near the easel, wiping up each drop of paint that goes astray, children are likely to feel less competent and take fewer risks in learning. I once observed a teacher who was great with insects, farm units, and birds. But whenever the children played with water or sand, she was visibly unsettled. I watched her one morning sweeping up sand as soon as it fell from the sand table. She hovered around the water table with towels, wiping up every drop that hit the floor. She always smiled at the children. She never said, "Careful! Careful! Don't spill the water! Don't let the sand fall!" Her constant vigilance, however, gave off a strong message of nonacceptance. The children in this room did not use the sand and water tables much. It wasn't possible for them to feel competent there in the face of this teacher's behavior.

When children are subjected to expectations beyond their abilities during this stage, they have no way of knowing that adult goals for them are inappropriate. They may respond in either of two ways. They may decide subconsciously that they must not be very capable and give up on the task. Or they may push themselves beyond their capabilities and succeed against the odds. These children mind all the rules, meet all the expectations, and seem to manage just fine. "What's wrong with this? Is there really a problem with overachievers or diligent workers?" you might be asking. The problem is that often these children learn that their value is measured by *what* they do rather than by *who* they are. Their initiative has not been damaged, but they still may carry a heavy load of feelings of guilt and inadequacy. They pay an emotional price for their success at adapting to unreasonable expectations.

Judith Warner's book *Perfect Madness: Motherhood in the Age of Anxiety* documents the pressure contemporary middle-class parents in the United States feel to "help" their children succeed in an overly competitive academic and social arena. Not only are these parents placing unreasonable expectations on their very young children, but they are compounding it by doing their children's homework or "helping" rather than letting their children develop at their own pace. According to Erikson's theory and more contemporary writers like Warner and Young-Eisendrath, this is a recipe for disaster.

To support children's development of initiative in the third stage, Erikson says that teachers can

- encourage children to be as independent as possible;
- focus on gains as children practice new skills, not on the mistakes they make along the way;
- set expectations that are in line with children's individual abilities; and
- focus curriculum on real things and on doing.

Encourage Independence
As with Montessori, teachers who apply Erikson's understanding of young children's development to their daily work with children will create classrooms where children can do things for themselves. Materials and equipment will be easily accessible to children, organized in ways that make it possible for them to both find what they need and put it away when they're done. Children will know where to find pails and sponges and paper towels to clean up messes when necessary. Family-style meals offer children opportunities to serve

70

themselves, to pour from pitchers even if they spill, and to clean up their places when they are finished.

Focus on Gains, Not Mistakes

According to Erikson, preschool children need the confident message from us that we take their initiative seriously. They need to know that their work is far more important than their messes or their mistakes. For example, one year I observed a teacher named Susan who often said to the children she taught, "Life is a work in progress!" She understood that sometimes children need a place to set a project for a while until they decide to come back to it. She encouraged the children to write stories, and her five-year-old students knew what an editor was. They were not afraid to make mistakes because, after all, this was only a draft. Susan sometimes asked the other adults in the room how to spell a word, or what ten times eleven was, modeling that teachers don't know everything, need help from others, forget things, and make mistakes. She was quick to show the children the things she had learned by making mistakes. One day I heard her say confidently to the children, "I'm getting better at the computer. I practice every day. I notice that I don't make mistakes as often as I used to."

This kind of teaching, according to Erikson, supports children's sense of competence in learning and contributes to their development of a sense of purpose.

Consider Individual Differences

Teachers work hard to plan a curriculum appropriate to the ages of children they teach. But often it's easy to forget the day-to-day differences that children bring with them. For example, if four-year-old Keisha has a new baby brother at home, cooperating with others in a typically age-appropriate way might be too big a challenge for her right now. If the teacher expects Keisha to share her new book even though she has recently had to share her parents for the first time, Keisha is vulnerable to discouragement or guilt. Aware of Erikson's theory about children's development, the teacher might say, "Usually I would ask Keisha to share that with the class, but today I think she needs to have it all to herself." This approach shows the understanding that, according to Erikson, teachers must consider not only children's developmental stage but also the individual factors that control what they are capable of on any given day.

It is harder and harder to focus on individual differences as expected skills are pushed aggressively at earlier and earlier ages. It is, however, probably more important than ever that we heed Erikson's warning to do so.

Focus Curriculum on Real Things
Like Montessori, Erikson believed that children in the stage of initiative versus guilt need real tools and real tasks in order to develop their competence. For example, Corinne planned to make vegetable soup with her class of preschoolers. When the cook brought her butter knives for the children to use to chop vegetables, she explained that if the children tried to cut carrots and celery with butter knives, they would fail. Instead, she taught them how to use sharp knives carefully. The children did a great job cutting the vegetables with the sharp knives. They also experienced a boost in confidence as they demonstrated how capable they really were.

For the same reasons, it makes just as much sense to teachers who understand Erikson to use real tools in the woodworking area. When children are carefully taught how to care for the tools and how to use them safely, their sense of competence skyrockets.

Erikson in the Twenty-First Century

The past decade has seen more understanding of psychology, brain development, and human development than growth in all of the other foundational topics covered in this text. It is interesting that even twenty years ago we were only beginning to talk about "cross-discipline" studies and inter-discipline collaboration. Erikson was able to develop his stages from almost a purely psychosocial perspective. As I count the number of times I mention the work of sociologists, media experts, and others while revising this edition, I am astounded by the complexity that has been layered onto our work with children in the past few decades.

It is impossible today to contemplate psychosocial development without focusing on culture, community, health and wellness, and changing family structures. This is not to say that Erikson's work is now out-of-date and not helpful to our understanding of young children's emotional development. It is to say that we must apply that broader lens when we view the many variables. When Erikson did his foundational studies on stages of development, there was little in the way of sympathetic understanding of young children. He needed to encourage adults to hold infants for feeding since the United States was falling into the trend of bottle-feeding and Madison Avenue was pushing "bottle props" to free up mothers' time and hands. He reminded adults that infant trust begins when adults respond quickly to infant tears at a time when the popular press was telling adults that if the baby was clean and fed, she should be allowed to cry herself to sleep without parental attention. He urged parents to

It is impossible today to contemplate psychosocial development without focusing on culture, community, health and wellness, and changing family structures.

73

understand that two-year-olds needed to assert their independence and this would sometimes result in meltdowns. It was a time when Benjamin Spock was warning parents about their child ruling the home if strict measures were not taken. It was a time when parents of six-year-olds were excited when their children learned the ABCs in first grade—and no one still in diapers played the violin or took swimming lessons.

So once again we need to exercise caution and balance as we look at educational psychology and daily practices. Perhaps the newest piece of this puzzle is the growing body of knowledge about how extreme some of our practices with young children have become. Here I am referring to the changes observed by Polly Young-Eisendrath (2008) and others of parents striving to develop positive self-esteem at any cost, and children running many homes in the United States rather than parents, and how educational standards are taking a direction that well-trained educators know is contrary to healthy development of our young children. For those of you under the age of forty, the reference above stating that fifty years ago both parents and teachers were thrilled if first graders had learned their ABCs must be startling. For those of you who do not work on a daily basis in programs for young children, it must be shocking to think that young children frequently boss their parents around at the end of a day spent in child care. Children say where they will go for dinner and who will come for a playdate this weekend. Too frequently, those of us who do work every day with young children see parents buckle and give in to these demands.

Young families live in much more social isolation than most families in this country did a century ago. With both parents employed all day and maternity and paternity policies in this country being practically nonexistent, most parents don't have the opportunity to observe and live with their child all day long for more than a few weeks. This does not lend itself easily to feelings of competence as a dad or mom. Our teacher education programs for early educators need to increase the "family support" component of our curricula. We need to demand that schools focus on the developmental needs and the individual needs of young children and that developmentally appropriate practice in the early years be respected. For this reason, those of us who work in the field must stay abreast of the changes in society and pedagogy that affect our work. We must review the theoretical foundations of our discipline so we have the appropriate reasons and justification for individualized instruction, outdoor play, and other important pieces of children's growth and development, which are at risk in contemporary United States culture.

Discussion Questions

1. Sydney is twelve weeks old. The teacher who usually cares for Sydney is out sick. Sydney cries and cries. When her mom picks her up at child care, she is upset that Sydney is exhausted and fretful. She requests that Sydney have several providers rather than a primary caregiver because she does not want more long, hard days like today. What do you say? How is this related to Erikson's theories?

2. At a parent meeting, Samuel's dad complains that he was "well-behaved" when he was in the infant room. Now that he has moved to the toddler room, he is always shouting "No" and running away. He pushed his eighteen-month-old cousin this weekend and grabbed his truck, yelling "Mine!" Samuel's dad wants to know when you will teach these children to share and behave. What will you say? How can Erikson's theory of autonomy help you answer the question?

3. Madison is in your kindergarten class. So is her best friend, Ella. When Ella's grandma dies, you read *Nana Upstairs and Nana Downstairs* by Tomie dePaola. The children talk a bit about dying. Later in the week, Madison's mom comes in angry. She says these discussions have no place at school. She does not want Madison upset. "She is just now getting over the death of my grandmother!" she says. You know that Madison's great-grandmother was special to them because she raised Madison's mom. You assure her that Madison has shown no sign of stress, but her mom is still upset. What do you think this is about? What does it have to do with Erikson's theories? How can you help?

Suggestions for Further Reading

Coles, Robert, ed. 2000. *The Erik Erikson Reader.* New York: W. W. Norton & Company.

Erikson, Erik. 1968. *Identity: Youth and Crisis.* New York: W. W. Norton & Company.

Sousa, David A. 2006. *How the Brain Learns.* 3rd ed. Thousand Oaks, CA: Corwin Press.

Warner, Judith. 2005. *Perfect Madness: Motherhood in the Age of Anxiety.* New York: Riverhead Books.

Chapter 4: Jean Piaget

The teacher-organizer should know not only his own science but also be well versed in the details of the development of the child's or adolescent's mind.

—Jean Piaget

Biography

JEAN PIAGET WAS BORN in Neuchâtel, Switzerland, in 1896. He was a budding scientist at an early age, publishing a scholarly paper at the age of eleven. Throughout his long career he added over sixty books and hundreds of articles to his accomplishments. Although Piaget is frequently referred to as a psychologist, he was really an *epistemologist* (someone who studies the nature and beginning of knowledge). It is this piece of his work that has made Piaget a major contributor to the knowledge base of educational psychology. While others asked *what* children know or *when* they know it, Piaget asked *how* children arrive at what they know.

Like many of us, Piaget hadn't planned on a career of working with children. He received a doctorate in biology but never worked in that field. Instead, he turned to psychology. In 1919 Piaget traveled to Paris to study and took a job at the Alfred Binet Laboratory School. His job was to standardize the French version of a British intelligence test. While doing this work, Piaget began to notice similarities in the wrong answers children gave to questions at certain ages, and he began to wonder what thought processes they were using. This became the research question that would drive his life's work. He continued to pursue his interest in children and their thought processes until his death in 1980.

Piaget's work has been a primary influence in preschool programs in the United States since the 1970s. The volumes of Piaget's work provide an in-depth view of how children create knowledge. Unfortunately, much of his work is difficult to read and can be intimidating to busy teachers. In addition, Piaget's work has been criticized in recent years for limitations that have been challenged by current research. Specifically, many teachers think he focused too much on thought processes and not enough on children's feelings and social relationships with teachers and peers. Many also believe his use of unfamiliar terminology confuses the reader. In addition, because much of his observation was done on his own three children, critics say the work is not scientific research.

Nonetheless, Piaget's stages of cognitive development have created our overall view of how children think in their early years, just as Erikson's stages of psychosocial development have helped us understand how children develop emotionally. Teachers can accept that while some of Piaget's theories are not as true of young children as was once thought, his basic concepts still help us plan curriculum to challenge young children's minds. To dismiss his work because of its flaws would be a mistake. The most sensible words I've read about Piaget's contributions came from Elizabeth Jones, who writes:

> People in all times and places invent explanations for what happens to them, and all explanations have predictive power; they enable us to say, "See, I told you." In our culture we call our explanations science and pretend they're real, not invented. But scientific explanations

change, just as myth and superstition do, because even in physics, and certainly in psychology, they provide only partial explanations of the way things really happen. Learn them, use them, but don't take them too seriously. Nothing happens because Piaget says it does. Piaget says it does because it happens, and he was an unusually thoughtful observer and generalizer. All of us can grow in our ability to do the same. (1986, 99–100)

Piaget's Theories

While others of his time argued that learning is either *intrinsic* (coming from the child) or *extrinsic* (imposed by the environment or taught by adults), Piaget thought that neither position by itself explains learning. Rather, he thought that children's interactions with their environment are what create learning. He claimed that children *construct* their own knowledge by giving meaning to the people, places, and things in their world. He was fond of the expression "construction is superior to instruction" (Hendrick 1992, 476). By this he meant that children learn best when they are actually doing the work themselves and creating their own understanding of what's going on instead of being given explanations by adults. He was a student of Montessori's work and built on her idea that meaningful work is important to children's cognitive development. Like Montessori, Piaget believed children needed every possible opportunity to do things for themselves. For example, children might be interested in how things grow. If a teacher reads them a finely illustrated book on how things grow, this instruction will increase the children's knowledge base. But if the children have the opportunity to actually plant a garden at school, the process of digging, watering, observing, and actually experiencing growing things will help them to construct a knowledge of growing things that they cannot ever achieve merely by being read to and looking at pictures.

79

Like Dewey, Piaget believed that children learn only when their curiosity is not fully satisfied. He thought that children's curiosity actually drives their learning. According to Piaget, the best strategy for preschool curriculum is to keep children curious, make them wonder, and offer them real problem-solving challenges, rather than give them information. Many adults still hold the notion that a teacher is someone who shares information. Using Piaget's theory about children's learning requires changing the image of *teacher* into someone who nurtures inquiry and supports the children's own search for answers.

Using Piaget's theory about children's learning requires changing the image of teacher into someone who nurtures inquiry and supports the children's own search for answers.

Piaget also stressed the importance of play as an avenue for learning. As children engage in symbolic play (making a cake out of sand, using a garden hose to be a firefighter), they make sense of the objects and activities that surround them. As they imitate what goes on around them, they begin to understand how things work and what things are for. Initially, this is a process of trial and error. However, with time and repetition, they use new information to increase their understanding of the world around them.

Piaget believed that children all pass through the same stages when developing their thinking skills. The age at which children accomplish these stages of development can vary. Because of this variation, charts outlining Piaget's stages may also differ slightly. Parents and teachers should always remember that individual children have their own rates of development. Differences in development stretch over a broad continuum. For example, many books cite ten to thirteen months as a typical age range for first steps. Yet some children walk as early as eight months and others as late as eighteen months.

Many teachers and other adults wonder if there are things that prevent growth or if there are ways to hurry development along. Piaget believed that children's intellectual growth is based partly on physical development. He also believed that it is affected by children's interactions with the environment. He did not believe that teachers can "teach" young children to understand a concept. He was certain that children build their own understanding of the world by the things they do.

According to Piaget, children's cognitive development passes through the stages shown in the following chart. After the chart is a basic discussion of Piaget's first two stages in children's journey to build knowledge, since these are the stages that most concern teachers in early care and education settings.

Piaget's Stages of Cognitive Development		
Age	**Stage**	**Behaviors**
Birth to age 2	Sensorimotor	Learn through the senses; learn through reflexes; manipulate materials.
2–7 years	Preoperational	Form ideas based on their perceptions; can only focus on one variable at a time; overgeneralize based on limited experience.
7–11 or 12 years	Concrete Operational	Form ideas based on reasoning; limit thinking to objects and familiar events.
11 or 12 years and older	Formal Operational	Think conceptually; think hypothetically.

(Piaget 1973)

81

The Sensorimotor Stage

Piaget believed that in the beginning, babies' reactions to the world are purely *reflexive* (without thought). He said that intelligence began when the reactions became purposeful. For example, when we watch an infant lying below a crib gym, we notice that initially he shows a startled response if his hand or foot hits a bell or rattle, but that, over time, he hits the bell on purpose. This first stage of cognitive development Piaget calls the *sensorimotor* stage. During this time the baby relies on his senses and physical activity to learn about the world.

Toward the end of this first stage, Piaget says, *object permanence* occurs. *Object permanence* means that the baby has come to realize that something exists even when he can't see it. This is a very important development for children. Before achieving this milestone, babies only think about what is in their view at the time. For example, if we carefully watch babies, we see that before eight or nine months they drop things from the high chair tray without making a fuss. For a young baby, if things are out of sight, they are literally out of mind. From the baby's point of view, the things no longer exist. Then suddenly, at eight or nine or ten months, when that spoon drops from the tray, the baby leans over pointing and fussing and wanting it back. Often parents and providers are surprised and dismayed when they pick it up and hand it to a smiling baby who tosses it right back down again. This is not the beginning of premeditated attempts to drive adults crazy. This is the first burst of the joy of learning! This is object permanence.

This is also the age at which we see *separation anxiety* in children. They cry when their parents leave them at child care or when their primary caregiver is not present. Now the baby understands that when his parent or provider is not in sight, that person is somewhere else. The caregiver hasn't just ceased to exist. So the baby makes attempts to bring that important "other" back into view—by crying.

To support cognitive development in children under two, Piaget's theory tells teachers to keep babies safe but interested and to respond reassuringly to separation anxiety.

Keep Babies Safe but Interested
Since motor development is a significant learning task of the sensorimotor stage, one of the most important supports to cognitive development that infant/toddler teachers can establish is a safe and interesting environment. Babies need to push, pull, and manipulate objects. They need to crawl, climb, and pull up to standing positions without being physically at risk. An infant environment with multilevel furnishing and climbing opportunities allows babies the spaces they need to experiment with spatial relationships and learn through their bodies. According to Piaget, babies also need interesting things to touch and explore. A variety of cause-and-effect toys (toys that make noise when pushed, pulled, or shaken) such as crib gyms and shape sorters are essential. Babies also need to have experiences with softer materials, such as nontoxic playdough, cornstarch-and-water, water, and sand. Mirrors and artwork at babies' eye level and board and cloth books that children can access provide even more interesting possibilities.

Babies' cognitive development is also stimulated by adults who talk with them and tell them what will be happening, and who delight in their accomplishments. Comfortable places for adults working in infant/toddler programs help them focus on the children and invite them to sit at the babies' level to provide another essential kind of interaction.

Respond Reassuringly to Separation Anxiety
When infants are beginning to experience object permanence and thus separation anxiety, it is important to make as few

changes in their lives as possible. With a little experience, they will begin to see that when people they love go away, those people always return. But during the transition time, it's a good idea to keep schedules routine. For example, this is not a good time to make new child care arrangements. Providers who understand this stage can help parents see why their babies are suddenly more upset than usual when they say good-bye. They can reassure parents that this stage, too, will pass if they can just give it a little time.

The challenges of separation anxiety have implications not only for how children are handled in the program but for enrollment policy as well. For example, Gini was the director of a center I supervised. She told me about holding an intake interview with parents who were considering moving their child from another provider into her center. She listened sympathetically as parents described tearful separations every morning from their ten-month-old baby. The parents were certain that their child must not like his current child care arrangements but couldn't tell them that because he wasn't yet talking. Gini talked with them about separation problems and encouraged them to wait another month or two before making any changes. She suggested that the baby would probably pass through this stage and be fine. The parents thanked her and left. A week later, she heard at a directors' meeting that the baby had been taken out of his current situation and enrolled at another nearby center. She was disappointed because she knew that the baby would now suffer even greater separation anxiety that probably could have been avoided if the other center's policies had supported children's developmental needs and if the family had chosen to wait a bit.

Providers can also support parents at this stage of development by welcoming them to call at any time to see how their child is doing and by acknowledging how hard it is for parents to walk away when their child is screaming. If parents

84

are anxious, their babies will share that anxiety, which makes everything worse. Everything teachers can do to reassure parents during this stage of infant development will support the growth of the babies in their care. Some programs don't even wait for parents to call but initiate the exchange because they understand how stressful it is for parents to be away from their babies. Sometimes parents get locked into a guilt reaction when their infant screams at separation in the morning. A quick call to say the baby's doing fine and share a story about the morning often makes the day easier for parents. When parents are supported in these ways, they are more apt to be able to maintain consistent schedules for their babies, which will help the babies get through separation anxiety more quickly and successfully.

During the earliest months of life, caring for parents is a big part of supporting children's development. New parents are under stress. Some mothers have anxiety because they need to return to work before they are ready to leave their babies. Some mothers wish they could stay at home but can't afford to. Others are eager to return to work but feel guilty and conflicted about doing so. Piaget's concept of object permanence and the separation anxiety that often accompanies it is not something most young parents know about. When teachers help parents understand their children's development, they are helping parents support that development.

The Preoperational Stage

According to Piaget, after the sensorimotor stage, children's cognitive development enters the *preoperational* stage, which extends from the second year of life through age seven or eight. The preoperational stage is when children's thinking differs most from adult thought patterns. Piaget said that during the preoperational stage, children are *egocentric* (think of everything only as it relates to them), can focus on only one characteristic of a thing or a person at a time (for example, take words at their exact meaning), gather information from what they experience rather than from what they are told, and overgeneralize from their experience.

Egocentrism means seeing the world from only one's own point of view. When observing preschoolers, adults frequently hear conversations like this one:

TEACHER: I've brought in many beautiful things for our blue display. We have blue paint at the easel, and I've put "Rhapsody in Blue" in the CD player since we are having Blue Day!

CHILD 1: My mom's car is blue.

CHILD 2: My mom's car is broke.

CHILD 3: My TV is broke.

TEACHER (TO CHILD 1): Your mom's car is blue?

CHILD 1: I saw lions on TV.

These children are typical of this developmental stage. This is the egocentrism Piaget refers to. The children are not connecting with each other's stories; rather, each child's words trigger other children's thoughts about their own situations. Another familiar example of egocentrism in young children is the child who wants to buy a stuffed toy as a gift for a parent or grandparent. Because this would please the child, she believes her grandfather will also love it!

Piaget believed that in the preoperational stage, children form ideas from their direct experiences in life. This is why telling children something is less effective than finding a way to help them think their own way through a problem. For example, if a child sees birds fly away when a dog barks, she may decide that barking dogs are the cause of birds' flight. Even though this is not an accurate idea, the child will be perfectly comfortable with her own reasoning despite any attempt to tell her otherwise. It is only after she has gathered more experience on her own—seeing birds take flight when no dog is around—that she will go through a mental process that challenges her worldview. Piaget calls this process *disequilibrium.* The child has to change her view and adapt it to her new information. Piaget calls the process of adapting one's understanding on the basis of new information *accommodation.* Accommodation returns the child to a more comfortable balanced state that Piaget calls *equilibrium.*

Piaget believed that in the preoperational stage, children form ideas from their direct experiences in life.

Because preoperational children tend to believe what they see, they do not yet have a firm grasp of qualities belonging to the objects in their world. For example, they confuse "heavy" with "large." Due to inexperience, most young children would initially be surprised that a beach ball is lighter than a baseball. Unable to separate height from age, preoperational children will insist that the tallest person is the oldest. Piaget did a classic experiment involving a *conservation task* to demonstrate this kind of thinking in children. He put two sets of coins on a table in two lines. Both sets had the same small number of coins, but the coins in one line were spread farther apart. When asked which line had more coins in it, preoperational children always said the line in which the coins were spread farther apart had more. They held to this belief even when the coins from the two lines were matched up to show that for each coin from the long line, there was a coin from the short line. *Conservation tasks* such as this one involving conservation of number show whether a child has grasped the concept that certain physical characteristics of objects remain the same, even though their outward appearance changes.

Because children at this stage are dependent on their own experience, they tend to make incorrect generalizations. They base their general belief about something on a single experience, which may cause a false conclusion. One example is the girl above who believed that a dog's barking made birds fly because she had seen birds flying when a dog barked.

Another instance is the child in a Virginia child care center whose parents told the teachers that he yelled and screamed on the weekend when they attempted to take him for a haircut. "He was hysterical and kept saying it would hurt too much!" the frustrated mother told the teacher. The teacher, who knew a great deal about young children and a little bit about Piaget, slowly explained to the mom that from her son's perspective there was good reason to be afraid of a haircut. By the age of three or four most youngsters have had enough experience with "boo-boos" to know that a *cut* on your knee or your finger can hurt quite a bit and sometimes even make you bleed. They know that at preschool, when they make soup, the teachers are very careful to show them how to chop the vegetables so they don't get *cut.* They know that Grandma doesn't let them use her good scissors because they might get *cut.* And then the grown-ups say they're taking you to get your hair *cut!* The child was overgeneralizing from his limited experience, and when his mother saw the situation from his perspective, his behavior suddenly made more sense to her.

Preoperational children also tend to focus on one attribute of an object or person at a time. It is hard for them to think of their mother as their grandma's daughter, for instance. This single-focus thinking is revealed in children's conversations, if adults know how to listen for it. For example, a Head Start teacher tells the story of a little girl in her class whose mom has had a new baby. The teacher shows the children pictures of babies in books. The children discuss how wrinkly and funny-looking babies are when they are born. The teacher tells the children that she heard one boy tell his mother that she should iron the baby. None of the children laugh at this or show any alarm. No one says, "Oh, that is awful. That would hurt the baby."

Instead, Kylie says, "My big sister irons her hair to get the curls out."

Joshua says, "That's not what it's for. You do it to get the lines off your clothes."

Clearly, the children do not make the connection that an iron might be a good tool to use on clothes or curly hair but not on babies. These children are not cruel or limited, but they are incapable of holding several qualities of an object or situation in their minds simultaneously. They are focusing on one aspect of the baby—the baby has wrinkles, and one aspect of the iron—the iron is used to get wrinkles out. The children do not naturally consider at the same time that the iron is hot, hot enough to hurt, and that a baby has skin like theirs that could be burned.

The teacher, aware that she has overestimated the children's understanding, can ask questions that make them think a little more about irons. "Is the iron you use on clothes hot?" she might ask. "How would you feel if you put it next to your skin? Does a baby have skin? How do you think it would feel to the baby's skin?" The children would quickly work out for themselves that an iron is not a good way to get rid of a newborn's wrinkly skin! Piaget's theory tells us that it will be more effective to ask questions that help children think through the problem on their own than to tell them flat out, "An iron would hurt the baby." If they *construct* that knowledge for themselves by puzzling through the teacher's questions, they are more apt to take it in than if the teacher gives it to them.

This characteristic of only seeing one aspect of a thing at a time also plays out in the way children this age take adults very literally. For example, Betty cared for her three-and-a-half-year-old niece Alison for a weekend. She invited Alison to help her with dinner preparations. At home, Alison's mother served her hot dogs on a roll with ketchup already on it. When Betty asked her niece to get the ketchup, Alison asked, "Should I put it on our hot dogs?" Betty, busy in the kitchen, responded, "No, just put it on the table." Betty was surprised when Alison squirted ketchup right onto the dining room table—just as she'd been told to do.

Teachers wanting to support the cognitive development of preoperational children in their care can

- provide large blocks of time for uninterrupted free-play time,

- provide many real-world experiences for children throughout the year, and

- plan open-ended activities and ask open-ended questions.

Provide Large Blocks of Free-Play Time

It is largely the influence of Piaget, building on Montessori's work, that encourages uninterrupted periods of play in early childhood classrooms. When children are interested and involved, they need teachers who respect this absorption with their work. Giving a child a little more time while others clean up for snack can be a way of saying, "I see that you are very involved with your work, and that is important." Sometimes it isn't necessary to completely clean up the room. Children need places where their ongoing work and projects can be left until they are ready to finish them. In times past, children often had abundant opportunities for this kind of ongoing work in their neighborhoods and backyards. It is now our responsibility to meet these needs for sustained projects and "works in progress" in our child care classrooms. When children are allowed large blocks of time for sustained interest in their play and work, teachers usually get more time to work one-on-one with those who need it.

It isn't necessary to insist that the whole group of children come together for a group time when three or four are having trouble finding an appropriate focus for their energy. Those children can do something else during group time. Many teachers are finding that times like snack and story time work much better when they are done in several shifts of small groups of children rather than groups of ten or twelve or eighteen, with some of the children unable to focus on the task at hand. Organizing to do small-group work simultaneously while others enjoy extended free-play time is how some teachers are making opportunities for more project work for those who are really engaged.

Time outdoors is another gift that teachers can share with children. The natural world provides young children with just as many opportunities to learn and grow across all developmental domains as the indoor classroom. While it is easy to say that time outdoors should be as rich and meaningful for children as the time spent in the classroom, this is not often the case. Just as teachers need to learn what to do with children indoors to create rich learning experiences for them, they also need to learn what to do with children outdoors. Many teachers are afraid to let children stay outside on a beautiful day because they fear it will be perceived as "doing nothing." However, the issue is not that the children are doing nothing when they are outdoors, it's that they could be doing—and learning—so much more. When children have regular opportunities to spend time in natural spaces, they learn about the world they live in and, just as important, come to understand the importance of taking care of it.

Many teachers today are frustrated by learning standards that are not developmentally appropriate for the ages of the children they teach but are pushed on them by school districts and state offices. The current age of accountability holds many positive things for teachers and children. For too many years, as discussed in almost every chapter, teachers have misinterpreted *progressive education* or developmentally appropriate practice (DAP) as letting the children do whatever suits them. This has resulted in much random wandering and many missed learning opportunities for children. Without careful planning, observation, and documentation, we cannot achieve meaningful curriculum. Accountability that requires observation and documentation stands to help us strive for excellence. It encourages us to help all the children to be all that they can be.

The problems arise when standards are driven by motives other than what is best for children. Standards requiring all kindergarten children to be reading at a certain level before entering the first grade are both unfair to individual children and unachievable by most teachers.

Reflecting on this aspect of teaching today can help all teachers to help children and each other to develop coping strategies for dealing with these unrealistic pressures. Talking with each other and with parents about the importance of taking time to learn is a good place to start. Sharing information with parents can help them to see that reading and other academic skills should not come at any cost or prior to a certain level of competence at prereading skills.

Provide Real-World Experiences
Like Montessori, Piaget has helped teachers of young children to see how important it is for children to experience whatever we want them to learn about. Looking at pictures of cows does not give a child the experience of cow—its size, smell, and sound, its function in our lives. Visiting a dairy farm, smelling the barnyard and the mown hay, watching machines milk the cows, and seeing the milk loaded into a truck gives children a completely different understanding of cows. Similarly, reading about "things that go" is not a substitute for riding on the

subway, in a taxi, in a bus, or on a train. Providing real-life experiences doesn't have to mean going on field trips. It can be as simple as cooking with children, bringing animals into the classroom, or studying the birds in your area as Kathy's class did in the chapter on Dewey.

It is possible anywhere to find real-life projects for children even if child care program resources are not what they could be. In rural New Hampshire, a team of Head Start teachers on a very limited budget did a project with children on building. They visited a lumber site and watched trees being cut and processed. They went to a construction area where a neighbor was having a house built, and then they realized they knew

Like Montessori, Piaget has helped teachers of young children to see how important it is for children to experience whatever we want them to learn about.

very little about the building their school occupied. The custodian became very involved. Children viewed the plumbing and electrical systems in the school. They did tracings of brick surfaces, floors, and other areas. The play that went on in woodworking and blocks showed a much deeper understanding of many construction principles than one usually views in a preschool room. This is what *construction of knowledge* is all about for young children.

Plan Open-Ended Activities, Ask Open-Ended Questions
Open-ended activities do not have a predetermined result or product. For example, when a teacher plans a science experiment to which she already knows the answer, the experiment is not open-ended. However, when children plant seeds and chart the days until the shoot breaks through the earth, and then measure the seedling every day and keep a graph of how it grows, the project is open-ended. Neither the adult nor the child knows what the result will be.

Similarly, open-ended questions do not have a predetermined answer. "What color is your shirt?" is a closed question. There is (probably) only one right answer, and the teacher knows what it is. "How do you think that works?" is an open-ended question. The teacher is asking the child for his reasoning and doesn't already know the answer.

Open-ended activities and questions support children's cognitive development because they ask children to think. Instead of putting children in the position of being right or wrong, they put them in the position of inquiry, of finding out what the possibilities are, like how fast the bean sprout grows. They help children look at several aspects of the same thing, as the teacher's questions about the hot iron and the baby's skin helped those children think about the consequences of ironing a baby. They help children accommodate new information. For example, take the child who thinks that a dog's barking makes the birds fly. Over time, an adult who knew that she had formed this idea about the world could help her adjust it by noticing dogs barking and birds flying, and asking careful open-ended questions such as, "I heard that dog bark behind the house, and look, those birds are sitting on the fence. Why do you suppose that is?" or "Look, there's a group of ducks taking off from the pond. Did you hear any dogs barking? Why do you suppose those ducks took flight?"

The Concrete Operational and Formal Operational Stages
The last two stages in Piaget's theory refer to school-age children and teenagers. Since the focus of this book is on the early childhood years, the discussion of these stages is very brief. It is helpful to all parents and teachers to know a little bit about these final stages. For more information, see the suggested reading list at the end of the chapter.

94

When children enter Piaget's stage of *concrete operations* at about age seven, many changes in their thought patterns are visible. At this age (usually from about seven through eleven or twelve) children possess the characteristic of *reversibility,* which allows them to reverse the direction of their thought. For example, a child at this stage can retrace her steps on the school yard looking for a forgotten lunch box. Children no longer count on their fingers because they are beginning to be able to think abstractly. They begin to notice differences in classes of objects. For instance, at four every dog is a "doggie," but at eight or nine there are differences between a collie and a poodle. The concrete-operational child can hold several qualities in mind, knowing that a boat is large, red, *and* a sailboat. She knows and really understands that her mother is also the daughter of her grandmother. With this new flexibility of thought, children can add, subtract, and multiply "in their heads."

The final stage Piaget outlined is *formal operations.* This stage begins around age eleven or twelve and is marked by the ability to think logically and in hypothetical terms. According to Piaget, once this stage is reached, young people can wrestle with such questions as "Is it wrong to steal food for your starving children?" or "If a tree falls in the forest and no one is there to hear it, does it make a sound?"

Piaget in the Twenty-First Century

It is interesting that Piaget and Erikson were peers and yet, in some ways, the changes to Piaget's work seem minimal compared to the psychosocial adaptations we need to make in the twenty-first century when pondering children's development. The quote from Elizabeth Jones at the beginning of the chapter is still so relevant to approaching theory over time. The foundational theorists of our field gave us such direction in understanding the developmental needs of young children that they are not diminished or discredited by changes in

The foundational theorists of our field gave us such direction in understanding the developmental needs of young children that they are not diminished or discredited by changes in society or knowledge that force us to make adaptations to their original work.

society or knowledge that force us to make adaptations to their original work.

I've seen and talked with many others who have also seen in recent years a capacity for *empathy* in young children that Piaget implied was not consistent with their developmental egocentrism. I like to think of this as a positive indication that more young children are getting their attachment needs met in infancy. Erikson asserted that meeting those needs consistently in infancy would result in a greater capacity for empathy.

What strikes me in reviewing Piaget's thorough description of the thought processes of the young child is how poor a match these developmental traits are for a preschool, kindergarten, and primary grade curriculum that insists on large group instruction with leveled expectations for all children. His work is the natural predecessor to project approach, emergent curriculum, differentiated instruction, and multiple intelligences. It does not seem a good fit for No Child Left Behind expectations in the United States. I'm not sure what to say about that.

I have always been fond of stating I like to raise questions, not necessarily provide answers. I think that Piaget's work is valid in guiding us to appropriate curriculum strategies for early education. Given the "pushed down" expectations of most standards for kindergarten and primary school curriculum into prekindergarten and preschool, I am leaning toward telling my daughter who will be teaching kindergarten next year to find a poster popular in her school district, put it on her door, and close her door. Then do what she knows is best for young children . . . but I'm not sure!

Discussion Questions

1. One of the nine-month-old babies in your infant program has always transitioned easily in the morning. You can tell from several clues that he has recently achieved object permanence. He begins to fuss and cry at separation from his parents in the morning, and they are alarmed at what they see as evidence that he is no longer happy in your program. You are convinced that his recent "clinginess" is related to his development. How can you explain this to the baby's parents?

2. Kevin is a four-year-old in your preschool class. He is very interested in building. He wants to spend all of his time in the block area. Kevin's mom worries that he plays too much. She has asked you to teach him math and language skills. Drawing on Piaget's work, how can you respond in a supportive way to this parent?

3. On a trip to the children's museum with your class of three-year-olds, a parent volunteer approaches you with one of the children in hand and says, "I just caught this one shoplifting!" How do you handle this situation? What do you say to the parent? What do you say to the child? How do you talk to the museum staff? How can Piaget's theories help explain what has happened?

Suggestions for Further Reading

Forman, George E., and David S. Kuschner. 1983. *The Child's Construction of Knowledge: Piaget for Teaching Children.* Washington, DC: National Association for the Education of Young Children.

Furth, Hans. G., and Harry Wachs. 1975. *Thinking Goes to School: Piaget's Theory in Practice.* New York: Oxford University Press.

Singer, Dorothy. G., and Tracey A. Revenson. 1996. *A Piaget Primer: How a Child Thinks.* Rev. ed. New York: Plume.

Chapter 5: Lev Vygotsky

Learning and development are interrelated from the child's very first day of life.

—Lev Vygotsky

Biography

LEV VYGOTSKY WAS BORN in Russia in 1896. His family was part of Russia's middle class, and they encouraged his studies. Vygotsky graduated from the University of Moscow in 1917 with a specialization in literature. He then taught literature in secondary school. This experience intensified his interest in teaching and in how people learn. He was particularly interested in cognitive and language development and their relationships to learning. This led to his interest in psychology and its impact on educational theory. Vygotsky studied and responded to the work of contemporaries Sigmund Freud, Jean Piaget, and Maria Montessori. He searched for answers to the questions raised by his interest in children and their approach to learning new things. That search led to his discovery: in a group of children at the same developmental level, some children were able to learn with a little help while other children were not. This piece of Vygotsky's learning is a cornerstone for the theories he developed.

It is hard to say what impact Vygotsky's perspective could have brought to our field with the passage of time. His brilliant career was cut short when he died of tuberculosis in

99

1934, at the age of thirty-eight. Many believe that his impact on educators in the United States was overshadowed by the huge popularity of Piaget's theories (Andrade and May 2004), which were enthusiastically embraced in preschools in the 1960s and continue to guide many classroom practices today.

More recently, many early childhood educators in the United States and other countries have turned their attention to the preschools in Reggio Emilia, Italy. Discussion of the educational theories implemented there has brought about a new focus on Vygotsky's work. Vygotsky's sociocultural perspective, for example, provides a theoretical basis for the Reggio-inspired approach to early childhood education.

Vygotsky's Theories

Vygotsky's ideas were and continue to be controversial. Because he came to the field without specific training in psychology and development, he brought a fresh perspective to child study. He objected to the analysis of children's abilities based on intelligence tests. He thought research should be both qualitative and quantitative. By this he meant that careful observation (qualitative research) of children should be considered as valid as their scores on a test (quantitative research).

Vygotsky has changed the way educators think about children's interactions with others. His work shows that social and cognitive development work together and build on each other. For years, early educators, schooled in Piaget's theories, viewed children's knowledge as being constructed from personal experiences. Although Vygotsky also believed this, he thought that personal and social experience cannot be separated. The world children inhabit is shaped by their families, communities, socioeconomic status, education, and culture. Their understanding of this world comes, in part, from the values and beliefs of the adults and other children in their lives. Children learn from each other every day. They develop language skills and grasp new concepts as they speak to and listen to each other.

Like Piaget, Vygotsky believed that much learning takes place when children play. He believed that language and development build on each other. When children play, they constantly use language. They determine the conditions of the make-believe. They discuss roles and objects and directions. They correct each other. They learn about situations and ideas not yet tried. Vygotsky believed that this interaction contributes to children's construction of knowledge—to their learning. Vygotsky's primary contribution to our understanding of young children's development is his understanding of the importance of interaction with teachers and peers in advancing children's knowledge. Today's Reggio-inspired educators also believe that what children learn from their peers and from the materials in the classroom is as important as what they learn from their teachers.

Vygotsky has changed the way educators think about children's interactions with others. His work shows that social and cognitive development work together and build on each other.

The Zone of Proximal Development

One of the most important concepts of Vygotsky's theory is that of the *zone of proximal development*, or *ZPD*. Vygotsky defined this as the distance between the most difficult task a child can do alone and the most difficult task a child can do with help. He believed that a child on the edge of learning a new concept can benefit from the interaction with a teacher or a classmate.

The term *scaffolding* is used to name the assistance a teacher or peer offers a child. A house painter working on a house uses a scaffold to reach parts of the house that would otherwise be out of reach. In the same way, adults and peers can help a child "reach" a new concept or skill by giving supporting information. Vygotsky believed this could be done not only by the teacher but also by the child's peers who already possess the desired skill. Vygotsky believed that in order to scaffold well for children, teachers need to be keen observers.

He believed that a child on the edge of learning a new concept can benefit from the interaction with a teacher or a classmate.

He believed that teachers need to use those observations to determine where children are in a learning process and where they are capable of going, given their individual needs and the social context that surrounds them. He believed that from information gathered through observation, teachers can support children's learning. This is similar to Dewey's belief that teachers must use their greater knowledge of the world to help make sense of it for children.

Teachers who want to apply Vygotsky's ideas about ZPD and scaffolding in their early childhood programs can observe children carefully and plan curriculum that encourages children's emerging abilities, and pair up children who can learn from each other.

Observe Children Closely and Plan Curriculum Accordingly
Like Montessori and Piaget, Vygotsky placed enormous emphasis on the importance of observation. By carefully watching and listening, teachers come to know each child's development. According to Vygotsky, this is the only way for teachers to accurately assess what is within a child's ZPD at any time. This knowledge is essential to good curriculum planning.

Curriculum planning is perhaps the area most affected by Vygotsky's theory. Unlike Piaget, who thought children's

102

cognitive learning was more internal than interactive, Vygotsky believed that interaction had a huge impact on cognitive development. Until Vygotsky's work became better known in the United States, educators here who understood Piaget's theory hesitated to "push" children. Piaget believed that stages of cognitive development are tied to physical development. He thought that children at a particular stage of development are incapable of the reasoning that they will grow into at the next stage. This led teachers to plan curriculum that supported children at their current level of expected development without stretching their developmental limits.

Vygotsky, on the other hand, showed that children's cognitive development is affected not only by their physical development but also by their social surroundings and interactions. His idea of developmental readiness is more flexible than Piaget's because it encompasses the skills or ideas that children have not yet come to on their own but which they can acquire from the example of peers or adults. This theory encourages teachers to plan curriculum that extends children's knowledge and to scaffold their learning by putting them in situations where their competence is stretched.

Plan Challenging Curriculum to Stretch Children's Competence
Here's an example of a teacher focusing on the ZPD of Margaret, one of her students. It also illustrates how both the teacher and the child's peers quite literally scaffolded her learning and growth. I once visited a class whose project focus was on building. The children had talked about construction, looked at books about building, practiced using tools at the woodworking bench, and visited construction sites. After much research, the children drew up their own blueprints for a playhouse in their yard. The day I visited, they were working on roofing. I observed as the children, with help from their teachers, climbed onto scaffolding and began

to hammer shingles onto the roof. Margaret lingered around the construction site. She wanted to hammer nails. Judy, her teacher, said, "We are roofing today. If you would like to help, I can help you climb onto the scaffolding."

Margaret said, "No, I just want to hammer nails."

Judy was firm. "When you go back inside, you can use the woodworking bench, if you like. Right now we are roofing. If you don't want to help, there are many other choices."

I was troubled by this. My own training made me question this teacher's approach. It seemed rigid to me. I thought, "Why can't she just give the child a piece of wood, a hammer, and some nails? She could sit near the building project and hammer her nails." My initial response was to compare the teacher's words, "If you want to hammer, climb up the scaffolding and do some roofing," to instructions from teachers in days of old who told the kids to draw a tree and added, "Color the leaves green, the trunk brown, and the sky blue." I didn't get it. I continued to watch the roofers as they hammered away.

Now and then Judy dropped a comment such as "Yesterday, Peter was afraid to climb up on the scaffolding. He thought he couldn't hold on and hammer too." Margaret didn't budge from her spot though there were many interesting choices available in the yard. She continued to watch the roofers. Judy continued to watch her.

"When Ashanti first climbed up to work on the roof, she just watched for a while because she was so scared being up high that she couldn't concentrate on hammering too," Judy said quietly after a while. I noticed that Margaret's initial whining and tearfulness at being prevented from hammering had stopped. She was now very attentive to the roofers, who received periodic encouragement from their teacher.

"You're getting many shingles hammered in," Judy said. Margaret watched.

"I wonder," Judy finally said, "if Ashanti would hold your hand for a while to help you get used to being up high. Then maybe tomorrow you would feel like hammering too."

At this comment, Ashanti joined in, "C'mon, Margaret. I'll hold your hand. I was scared, too, before." Margaret stood up. Judy offered her assistance as Margaret climbed up the scaffolding. Ashanti held her hand once she got up. The look on her face changed from the sad, tentative, and displeased expressions she had worn all morning to one of utter triumph.

Overwhelmed by her accomplishment, Margaret's sense of competence exploded. "Gimme some nails!" she shouted joyfully. Margaret hammered her first shingle. Judy smiled. "A job well done!" she said. I learned a lot that day. I realized that, had I been Margaret's teacher, she'd have spent her morning happily "on the edges" of the building project. I'd have given her some nails, a board, and a hammer. She'd have been content to spend her time doing something she was comfortable with, without risking any new learning. At the end of the day, the child would have gone home much as she had arrived in the morning. Judy, however, sent home someone who had triumphed over fear, someone who had increased her skills and competence, which led to an increase in self-esteem. She had carefully observed her student and accurately judged that she was ready to take a leap with a little help. This is *scaffolding*. The skill of climbing the scaffold and hammering in the nails was within Margaret's ZPD. She wouldn't have done it on her own, but with help, she was able to achieve it.

It's important to recognize that using Vygotsky's ZPD requires careful observation of children and good judgment about how best to support their learning. Judy knew that Margaret was capable of doing the climbing and roofing. She knew that Margaret was afraid of being up high. She knew that Margaret would not choose to climb the scaffolding

105

without help. All of this observation and the resulting knowledge of the individual child is crucial to the successful scaffolding in this story. Without knowing each child well and taking the time for careful observation and reflection before making the move to urge a child further, teachers can make serious mistakes.

Here's another example of how ZPD can affect life in the classroom. Early in my teaching career, I had a five-year-old student named Lynn who did not want to fingerpaint. Lynn's mother did not like "messes." I wanted to "free" Lynn's creative spirits from her mother's tidy control! I refused to believe that she didn't want to fingerpaint. I'm sure I thought I was "guiding" not "forcing" when I took her little hands in mine and put both of them into the fingerpaint. When Lynn threw up all over the fingerpaint and both of us, I learned the hard way that not every child should experience fingerpainting. I had not listened carefully to my student. I had not observed enough. I was not respectful of her family's approach. I wanted to force an experience on her that I had decided would expand her horizons. Because I didn't know her individual needs, my plan backfired. Fingerpainting was not within Lynn's ZPD that day, and my attempt at scaffolding failed.

Language Development and Learning

Vygotsky believed that language presents the shared experience necessary for building cognitive development. He believed that talking is necessary to clarify important points but also that talking with others helps us to learn more about communication. We can learn much from observing children's conversations. It can help us find out what the children know and what they are confused about. Many of us have memories of schools where we were expected to be quiet and study. Teachers at the time thought learning was a solitary journey, something each student had to do alone. Vygotsky has shown us the importance of learning as an interactive experience. Teachers who want to encourage cognitive development can do it by encouraging conversations.

Encourage Conversations
Sometimes teachers still discourage conversation. Often this happens at group time. Teachers do presentations on topics such as growing things, dinosaurs, or transportation, hoping to share their knowledge of the world with children. Interruptions are considered a disruption to the "lesson." An understanding of Vygotsky's theory allows us to see the role of language—questioning, talking, joking, interrupting—in extending children's learning. In dramatic play, we frequently hear children adjusting their view of the world. For example, one day I overheard this conversation at a child care center:

JUAN: I'll be the nurse.

NICOLE: No, you can't! My mama's a nurse. You have to be a girl.

HEATHER: Yeah, the boys is supposed to be the doctors.

ERLEEN: The doctor that got my mom's baby out was a girl.

DYLAN: C'mon, Juan, just be a doctor so we can play this game!

Individual opinions are offered here. Experiences are shared. Dylan is even sophisticated enough to see that he and Juan are caught in a "word battle" and it's holding up the play. In this situation there is content learning (both men and women can be doctors) but also process learning (all this talking is getting in the way of play, but if we just agree, the play will go on!).

Many teachers would have cut this discussion short by jumping in at the first incorrect statement to make sure the children knew that men and women could be nurses. In the above situation, the teacher quietly concluded for the children as the conversation ended that it sounded as though they all knew different things about doctors and nurses, but that it was true that men and women worked at both jobs. By letting the children continue their arguments and discussions, she nurtured not only the content of the conversation but also the process, which will help them all become better learners.

Social Interaction

According to Vygotsky, interactive situations like the one described above allow children to stretch and grow mentally. Too often teachers have acted as if language and cognitive abilities will develop with little help or direction. But growing and learning does not necessarily happen "naturally." One teacher I knew from a previous generation used to say, "The children will grow taller without my help but not smarter or kinder!" Teachers need to develop the skills of observing, questioning, and encouraging peer interactions that will best support children's growth and development. They need to think about when to step in with suggestions or ideas and when to let the children proceed on their own.

Vygotsky's theory that development is interactive changes the way we think about children's learning. For some teachers, the idea that children can help each other learn is very freeing. They suspect that they have sometimes interrupted excellent opportunities for group learning to call children to circle time, where they must sit and listen. Vygotsky has helped teachers to see that children learn not only by doing but also by talking, working with friends, and persisting at a task until they "get it." To support children's social learning, teachers can provide many opportunities for children to help one another or to work together on projects of their choice.

108

Provide Opportunities for Children to Work Together

I saw a fine example of children working together one spring day in northern New Hampshire. It was a perfect example of a teacher allowing two children to learn from each other and their joint experience. The rural Head Start program at which I was observing had a wonderful outdoor play area. Nature had provided a perfect science center. Shady areas offered patches of ice for sliding. Sunny areas offered muddy puddles of melted snow. Long icicles hung dripping from the building's low roof. Children played in every corner of the yard. In the midst of all of this activity, two four-year-old boys found a treasure. Sticking out of some ice was the top of a mitten. They decided to "excavate" for the other half. First, they tried digging for it with twigs. After large, small, and medium-sized twigs had broken, they decided they needed "real" tools. The teacher unlocked a toolshed for them and observed their choice of tools. The boys brought out a shovel that was eighteen or twenty inches taller than either of them. "It's stuck in there hard, so we need something big to get it out," Kevin said. "Yup," Jeffrey agreed.

The teacher did not say, "That's too big" or "Someone will get hurt." She stayed nearby and watched. First, the boys argued about who should dig first. Then Jeffrey, predictably, knocked the handle into Kevin when he tried to use the shovel. "Let me," Kevin said. "You're not doing it right—you keep hitting me and not the mitten." He tried—with the same outcome, of course. The teacher said, "Wow, you guys are really working on that project." The boys grinned but said, "It's not going right. Maybe we need a smaller digger." The teacher said, "Uhmm, maybe so." So off they went, returning with a small gardening rake and shovel. These boys sustained their focus and energy on this task for about half an hour. They met with frustration and talked out loud to each other

109

and to themselves as they struggled. Eventually they got past taking turns and progressed to cooperation. They realized that one needed to dig while the other pulled.

When they finally got the mitten out, the wise teacher did not respond, "Good job." Here is what she offered instead. "You two worked really hard together. You tried many things. Some didn't work, but you didn't let yourselves feel discouraged. You kept trying other solutions. Together you worked it out. You must feel pleased with yourselves." This response to the children crystallized their experience and helped them understand it better by reflecting it back to them concretely and explicitly. This is another example of scaffolding.

The teacher increased the children's learning by not rushing in to give them answers. Through interaction, conversation, and experimentation, the children increased their skills and accomplished their goals. Through their interactions, they learned process—how to negotiate about using tools; how to experiment to see which tool works the best. And they learned content—what's the most effective way to dig a frozen object out of a patch of ice, and, incidentally, principles of physics such as leverage. Vygotsky believed that learning and development are similar but not identical. The combination of instructing the child and honoring the child's individual development optimizes learning.

Vygotsky believed that learning and development are similar but not identical. The combination of instructing the child and honoring the child's individual development optimizes learning.

Executive Function

There is growing evidence today that suggests that a preschool-age child's ability to apply cognitive control,

110

also called *executive function*, is a better predictor of later school success than any academic learning acquired during the preschool years. Executive function encompasses self-regulation skills, including social skills, self-discipline, and mental flexibility. Children who lack these skills, or mental tools, do not know how to learn in a deliberate manner—they are "unable to focus their minds on purpose, and consequently their learning is less effective and efficient" (Bodrova and Leong 2007, 5).

Until recently, it was generally assumed these skills were ones not easily taught in the early childhood classroom. However, new findings in brain research have established relationships between the development of self-regulation skills and the maturation of particular areas of the brain. The research suggests that as with many brain capacities, executive function can be built through practice. In addition, research shows that children develop the foundational skills for self-regulation in the first five years of life. These findings have many implications for early childhood education and highlight the important role teachers play in helping young children develop the critical skills associated with executive function.

Because self-regulation skills develop over time, it is important that teachers keep in mind each child's zone of proximal development and offer learning experiences that are in keeping with what each child is ready to learn (scaffolding), including experiences the child can practice with teachers and able peers. Teaching techniques that foster self-regulation skills include modeling appropriate behavior and providing hints and cues about how and when children should regulate their behavior. Only after a child has consistently demonstrated self-regulation skills on his or her own, or has *internalized* those skills, should teachers begin withdrawing support.

Foster Self-Regulation Skills through Make-Believe Play
While much is known about the positive effects of make-believe play on children's social, early literacy, and early

Only after a child has consistently demonstrated self-regulation skills on his or her own, or has internalized those skills, should teachers begin withdrawing support.

mathematical development, research has shown that make-believe play also has positive effects on the development of self-regulation skills in young children (Singer, Golinkoff, and Hirsh-Pasek 2006). Inherent in make-believe play is the zone of proximal development, because it is during this type of social play that children frequently behave beyond their years and above their everyday behavior. As children participate in make-believe play, they are practicing regulating behavior naturally—they regulate other children by telling them what to do; they regulate themselves by staying in their roles and trying not to do anything that might interrupt the flow of the play; and they are regulated by other children when they agree to roles and rules that may not be the ones they had in mind.

Here's a great example of this. It's Deerfield Fair week in New Hampshire. RVs and campers, horse trailers, and trucks pull into the fairgrounds. School closes on Friday because experience has taught the superintendent that nobody comes that day anyway. Everyone is at the fair.

When the children return to school on Monday, the teacher has transformed the dramatic play area into a campsite at the fair. The children are ecstatic and begin at once to process and relive their weekend's experiences. Josh (6), Pete (4½), Rachel (5), and Lynn (5½) are in the area together. Rachel and Lynn immediately head to the stove and start pulling out a huge variety of "vegetables" to cook. The girls feel a sense of "social dominance" over food preparation. Josh, self-assured and clearly full of ideas, starts laying some ground rules. "First," he says, "we need to decide who we are. We need to be married. I'll be married to you, Rachel."

Rachel thinks this is wrong. All of the children know each other's ages. "I should be married to Pete," she says (probably based on the fact that they are close in age). "No," Josh says. "She is the right size for Pete." (Lynn is older but smaller than Rachel.) Josh is really into the play. He turns from the girls to Pete. "Didja bring the beer?" he says comfortably. Pete giggles and shakes his head No. He looks at the teacher. He's not as sure of the "role play" (a perfect re-enactment). Pete thinks he's probably not supposed to talk about beer at preschool. Lynn, content to be part of the group, says nothing at all.

We can see the interactive nature Vygotsky describes in the children's play. Josh knew what to do immediately. He never questioned the appropriateness of his words, as they were supposed to be guys at the fair with their wives. Rachel rejected her suggested role, as she concluded age, not height, should make the match. Pete's behavior is a good indicator of self-regulation at work. He senses "beer" is not a school word but isn't quite sure. He's not as confident of his role in the play as Josh. Lynn listens as her eyes dart from one to the other of her peers. She is quiet, not comfortable speaking up in the setting, yet confident enough to do just what she wants to— enjoy watching and learning from the rest of her peers.

Teachers who want to apply Vygotsky's ideas about the ZPD and scaffolding to encourage rich make-believe play in their early childhood programs can

- ensure children have enough time for play;
- offer children appropriate toys and props; and
- observe children's play and, when appropriate, share ideas for themes that could enrich and extend their play.

113

Vygotsky in the Twenty-First Century

Vygotsky added a new voice to those of his founding peers when he suggested that interaction was as important to learning as constructing one's own ideas. His zone of proximal development was a startling addition to those of us taught a purely Piagetian approach to young children and learning. There was great emphasis for at least three decades ('60s, '70s, and '80s) on the importance of *not* pushing preschoolers. Initially, the notion of ZPD and taking children to the next possible step created an instinctive (or actually conditioned) cringe. We didn't want to push!

But it makes sense, and the idea took some pressure off teachers by suggesting that children often learn as much or more from a more-skilled peer than they do from their teachers. As we all tried to scaffold children's learning, we realized these ideas really do work. Then again, the pace of many preschool and primary grades these days doesn't leave much time for teachers to encourage conversation.

We have a responsibility to share Vygotsky's concept of the executive function's impact on self-regulation at a time when school districts are discouraging play and conversation in kindergarten. We know from many experiences that the guidance of our founding theorists is as important today as it was when they first laid out these ideas. So what are committed educators to do with the gaps between what we know is best and what is expected from us?

I suggest that every parent and teacher interested in the future of our society and education read Maggie Jackson's book *Distracted: The Erosion of Attention and the Coming Dark Age*. This will not be comforting in light of Vygotsky's work, as she suggests that the current generation of young children growing up on texting, Tweeting, Skyping, and using Facebook are less competent at verbal interaction than many previous generations. As pointed out in the chapter on Dewey, we cannot look progress in the face, judge it as detrimental, and turn the other way. There is no point. But Jackson's information gives us one more sobering piece of information to contemplate so that together we can all begin developing strategies to help young children speak to and learn from one another.

Discussion Questions

1. When your school district implements a K–3 primary program, some parents are upset that younger children will "hold back" the learning of their second and third graders. Using Vygotsky's sociocultural theory of development, tell parents how the new program will be good for all of the children.

2. Kimberly is a five-year-old in your preschool. Her parents want her to read before entering first grade. You've read David Elkind. He says, "Don't push children." You've read Vygotsky. He says if reading is in a child's ZPD, it's okay to push a little. You've read Piaget. He says play is the best way for children to learn. You have to decide how to work with Kimberly's family to help her make the transition to public school. What do you need to know about Kimberly before you decide what to do? What are some possible ways of handling the situation? How would you choose one?

3. Many primary-grade classrooms expect children not to "socialize" with other children during their class time. What would Vygotsky think of this practice? Why?

Suggestions for Further Reading

Berk, Laura E., and Adam Winsler. 1995. *Scaffolding Children's Learning: Vygotsky and Early Childhood Education*. Washington, DC: National Association for the Education of Young Children.

Galinsky, Ellen. 2010. *Mind in the Making: The Seven Essential Life Skills Every Child Needs*. NAEYC special ed. New York: HarperCollins.

Vygotsky, Lev. 1978. *Mind in Society*. Edited by Michael Cole et al. Cambridge, MA: Harvard University Press.

Glossary

accommodation: Piaget's term for the process of adapting one's understanding on the basis of new information.

attachment: According to Erikson, the bond between a young child and his parents and primary caregivers.

autonomy: The capacity to act independently.

concrete operations: Piaget's third stage of cognitive development, lasting from about six years to about twelve years of age, during which children use reasoning to make judgments.

conservation tasks: Classic experiments conducted by Piaget and associated with the preoperational stage that demonstrate whether a child knows that certain physical characteristics of objects remain the same even though their outward appearance changes.

construction of knowledge: The process by which a child creates a mental explanation for her experience or perceptions, according to Piaget.

disequilibrium: Piaget's term for a child's state of mind when her understanding of the world is being challenged by her experience, before she has created a new understanding to explain her new experience.

egocentric: Thinking of everything one encounters only as it relates to oneself; seeing the world from only one's own point of view.

Eight Ages of Man: Erikson's theory of psychosocial development, which covers the life span of human beings.

empathy: The ability to put oneself in another person's place and understand what he or she might feel.

epistemologist: A person who studies the nature and beginning of knowledge.

equilibrium: Piaget's term for the state of mind during which a child's experience in the world is adequately explained by her understanding.

executive function: Refers to the ability to manage or regulate basic cognitive and emotional processes, such as self-regulation, the ability to focus on tasks, the ability to organize thoughts and materials, and the ability to follow through and complete tasks.

extrinsic: Coming from without; imposed by something or someone else.

formal operations: Piaget's fourth stage of cognitive development, lasting from about twelve years of age through adulthood, in which people are capable of abstract, conceptual, and hypothetical thought.

identity crisis: Erikson's term for the conflict young people experience as they grow into adulthood.

intrinsic: Coming from within; an essential part of the nature of something.

learning experience: Dewey's term for an activity that meets five criteria: is based on the children's interests and grows out of their existing knowledge and experience; supports the children's development; helps the children develop new skills; adds to the children's understanding of their world; and prepares the children to live more fully.

mis-educative: Dewey's term for an activity that lacks sufficient purpose and organization to support children's learning.

object permanence: The point at which a baby realizes that objects exist even when he cannot see them, according to Piaget.

open-ended: An activity or question without a predetermined product or answer.

preoperational: Piaget's second stage of cognitive development, lasting from about eighteen months to about six years of age, during which children learn based on their perceptions and experience.

progressive education: A movement toward more democratic and child-centered forms of education and away from hierarchical and didactic instruction, beginning at the end of the nineteenth century.

reflexive: Without thought.

scaffolding: Term for the assistance a peer or adult offers a child that helps her learn a skill or develop knowledge she could not develop on her own.

sensorimotor: Piaget's first stage of cognitive development, lasting from birth through about eighteen months of age, in which children's growth in thinking is largely governed by what they perceive through their senses and what they learn through reflex movements.

separation anxiety: A child's reaction of distress to separation from a parent or primary caregiver.

zone of proximal development (ZPD): Vygotsky's term for the distance between the most difficult task a child can do alone and the most difficult task a child can do with help; the area of development a child has not reached on his own but that he can reach with the input of others.

References

Andrade, Jackie, and Jon May. 2004. *Instant Notes in Cognitive Psychology*. New York: Garland Science/BIOS Scientific Publishers.

Bodrova, Elena, and Deborah J. Leong. 2007. *Tools of the Mind: The Vygotskian Approach to Early Childhood Education*. 2nd ed. Upper Saddle River, NJ: Pearson Education, Inc.

CCSSO (Council of Chief State School Officers). 2012. "1990 National Teacher of the Year." Accessed July 23. www.ccsso.org/ntoy/ National_Teachers/Teacher_Detail.html?id=1142.

Chaillé, Christine, and Lory Britain. 2003. *The Young Child as Scientist: A Constructivist Approach to Early Childhood Science Education*. 3rd ed. Boston: Allyn & Bacon.

Coontz, Stephanie. 1992. *The Way We Never Were: American Families and the Nostalgia Trap*. New York: BasicBooks.

Dewey, John. 1899. *The School and Society*. Chicago: The University of Chicago Press.

———. [1915?]. *My Pedagogic Creed*. Chicago: A. Flanagan Company.

———. 1938. *Experience and Education*. New York: Collier Macmillan.

References

Erickson, Erik. (1950) 1963. *Childhood and Society.* 2nd ed. New York: W. W. Norton & Company.

Gerber, Magda, ed. 1997. *The RIE Manual for Parents and Professionals.* Los Angeles: Resources for Infant Educarers.

Hendrick, Joanne. 1992. *The Whole Child: Development Education for the Early Years.* 5th ed. New York: Merrill.

Jones, Elizabeth. 1986. *Teaching Adults an Active Learning Approach.* Washington, DC: National Association for the Education of Young Children.

Kagan, Jerome. 1998. *Three Seductive Ideas.* Cambridge, MA: Harvard University Press.

Louv, Richard. 2008. *Last Child in the Woods: Saving Our Children from Nature-Deficit Disorder.* Chapel Hill, NC: Algonquin Books.

Montessori, Maria. (1949) 1967. *The Absorbent Mind.* Translated by Claude A. Claremont. New York: Holt, Rinehart and Winston.

Nearing, Scott. 2007. *The New Education: Progressive Education One Hundred Years Ago Today.* New York: The New Press.

New Hampshire Pediatric Society Newsletter. n.d. "Media Violence and Medical Literacy."

Piaget, Jean. 1973. *The Child and Reality: Problems of Genetic Psychology.* Translated by Arnold Rosin. New York: Grossman Publishers.

Schor, Juliet B. 1991. *The Overworked American: The Unexpected Decline of Leisure.* New York: Basic Books.

Siegel, Larry J. 1998. *Criminology: Theories, Patterns, and Typologies.* 6th ed. Belmont, CA: West/Wadsworth Publishing Company.

Singer, Dorothy G., Roberta M. Golinkoff, and Kathy Hirsh-Pasek, eds. 2006. *Play = Learning: How Play Motivates and Enhances Children's Cognitive and Social-Emotional Growth.* New York: Oxford University Press.

Tanner, Laurel N. 1997. *Dewey's Laboratory School: Lessons for Today.* New York: Teachers College Press.

Young-Eisendrath, Polly. 2008. *The Self-Esteem Trap: Raising Confident and Compassionate Kids in an Age of Self-Importance.* New York: Little, Brown and Company.

125

culture, effect on growth and development, 5
curiosity, as driver of children's learning, 80
curriculum models, 19, 21
curriculum planning
  focus on real things, 72
  notion of paid time for, 30–31
  observation and reflection in, 18, 44, 46–48, 102–3
  open-ended activities in, 93–94
  purposeful, 19–22
  questions to ask, 26
  to stretch children's competence, 103–6

D

Death of the Grown-up, The (West), 49
developmentally appropriate practice (DAP), misinterpretation of, 92
developmental readiness, 103
Dewey, John
  agricultural to industrial age transition and, 31–32
  biography, 13–16
  on change, 15
  criteria for educational experiences, 26
  early childhood curriculum models, 19
  parents in early industrial age and, 14–15
  philosophy of education, 16–17
  progressive education movement and, 15–19
  on teachers' role in children's learning experiences, 17–19
  in the 21st century, 30–33
Dewey's Laboratory School, 14
discussion questions
  Dewey chapter, 33

Erikson chapter, 75–76
Montessori chapter, 50
Piaget chapter, 97
Vygotsky chapter, 115
disequilibrium, 87, 117
Distracted (Jackson), 114–15
documentation, organization and, 28–30

E

early childhood education, theoretical foundations, 9–10
Early Sprouts approach, 31
educational experiences, criteria for and teachers' role in, 17–19, 22, 26
educational psychology and theory, 14, 74
educational theorists, contemporary, 15
education vs. mis-education, 25–26
egg-blowing learning experience, 21–22
egocentric, defined, 117
egocentrism, in children, 85–86
Eight Ages of Man (Erikson), 54, 117
empathy, 57, 96, 118
employed hours, 6
environments for learning
  child-centered, 38, 40–42
  infant-centered, 83
  natural, 79
  outdoor play areas, 109–10
epistemologist, defined, 77, 118
equilibrium, defined, 87, 118
Erikson, Erik
  biography, 53
  Childhood and Society, 53, 55
  and children's capacity for empathy, 96
  context of foundational studies by, 73

126

Index